RAILROAD STORIES

The Story of Industrial America Series
1850's - 1950's
Volume One

RAILROAD STORIES

The Story of Industrial America Series
1850's - 1950's
Volume One
Jim Kissane

Cover Image Credit: [New Railroad], 1916, Frank and Frances Carpenter collection (Library of Congress).

"The Story of Industrial America" is a selection of historically inspired works describing people, places and events of several specific major American industries of the 1850's through 1950's.

Each volume is lavishly illustrated with archival photos and drawings and includes glossary of industrial terms and an extensive reading list along with author commentary on the sources for the stories.

Readers will enjoy volumes containing original short stories about Automobiles, Communications, Construction, Electricity, Iron and Steel, Logging and Lumber, Manufacturing, Material Handling, Meatpacking, Mining, Motor Trucks, Oil and Gas, Railroads, Textiles, Transportation, Trolleys and Inter-urbans, and a special selection about America's "Western Expansion" during this era.

ISBN: 979-8-9874326-1-7

This book was produced with editorial guidance and technical support from Self-Publishing Consultant Robin Moore. To learn more about gaining assistance on the pathway to publishing before a world-wide readership on the Amazon platform, visit: www.robin-moore.com

Gold foil art on cover from Vecteezy.com

CONTENTS

INTRODUCTION

DO YOU long for the "Glory Days of Trains" which took place during the mid-19th to the early 20th century?

If so, I know you will enjoy this collection of short stories I have created to celebrate an era of American Industrial history which no longer exists. Let me describe for you a magical time when the railroads were central to America's western expansion and were opening up our young country in ways that only a handful of visionary builders could have been imagined.

Today's railroads bear little resemblance to the railroads of the 1850's to 1950's. In these pages, you'll experience people and places where the railroad impacted their lives in very different ways.

I grew up in Elmira, a city in upstate New York that in the early 20th Century was a hub for five major railroads. On peak days, as many as one hundred and fifteen trains passed through our railyards.

My dad had worked for the Delaware Lackawanna & Western (DL&W), and my grandfather was employed by the Pennsylvania Railroad (PRR). In their roles, the two of them knew many railroad people.

I was delighted to be taken to visit the local rail yards with them. They would take me around and explain things about railroad life that only railroad people would know.

Their connections enabled me to get free rides in the cabs of steam and diesel locomotives and to ride at the end of the trains in the cabooses where I met the Conductors and Brakemen.

And with each person I met, I got to listen to their own experiences and stories.

That planted the seed for my love of railroads.

One of my early jobs in my career was working for General Railway Signal Company, a hundred year-old manufacturer of the railroad signaling and switching equipment that is used by all of the railroads.

Later, as a volunteer with the Railway Historical Society, I got the special opportunity to work with others involved with restoring vintage locomotives and rolling stock.

These folks helped get me involved with some people in my city who had the dream of restoring an abandoned rail line running through the heart of Pennsylvania's historic Oil Creek Valley. Those efforts culminated in the creation of the Oil Creek and Titusville Railroad (OC&T), a successful short line that today continues to provide tourist and freight service.

Over the years, my wife and I have served as Conductors on Steam Locomotive Excursions helping rail fans who wanted to enjoy a railroad experience that today is hard to find.

I would like to thank Nancy, my bride of many decades, for her continuous support and assistance in creating this work. I could not have created this book without her guidance, encouragement and assistance in editing and putting it together.

I hope you enjoy reading these stories as much as I have enjoyed sharing them.

A SECOND CHANCE

AFTER THE Civil War, soldiers on both sides often discovered they had no home awaiting them on their return and no job. Cletus was one of those men, now fifty-one years old, a career tramp with few marketable talents and limited prospects.

The War had ended his formal education and he had few useful skills other than manual labor. For the past twenty years, he had worked his way back and forth across the country, living a primitive nomadic lifestyle that his military experience had taught him, sometimes burning shoe leather, occasionally hopping on and off passing freight cars, living off the land, and taking whatever he could pilfer. If all else failed, he did a bit of menial work to get by from day to day.

Yesterday morning, Cletus had hitched a free ride on an outbound freight train leaving Chicago while a distracted brakeman was looking the other way.

His usual mode of rail transport involved riding underneath the car on the truss rods, but today he had spotted a boxcar with an open door and had crawled inside as it left the Chicago rail yard.

Riding the Truss Rods

After a more comfortable ride and a nice nap

inside the box car, he felt a familiar jolt and sensed that the train was slowing down.

Pushing aside the heavy door of the boxcar, he felt the morning sun beaming down on his face, and with it came a warm breeze, suggesting that today would be a hot one.

Taking a deep breath, the old tramp picked out an inviting spot and jumped from the car, rolling down the gentle embankment, ending up face-up in an overgrown patch of weeds.

As he lay there, staring up at the billowy clouds passing across the blue sky above, his stomach growled loudly, reminding him it had been almost eighteen hours since he had anything to eat.

"Say, friend, do you see that white house over there among the trees--the one with the porch and the flower beds in front? Well, if you go there, I promise you'll be treated well."

Cletus sat up with a start, unaware that there was someone nearby. As he looked around, there in the heavy brush was a younger man who continued, saying, "There's a woman living in that house who's never been known to turn a hungry man away from her door ---she'll give you the best she's got, and give it willingly, too."

That's all Cletus needed to hear.

Then, with a grunt, the younger man laid back down in the brush, and soon after that, Cletus heard him snoring loudly. Cletus's stomach was really growling now and his new friend had told him everything he needed to know. By the fifth snore, Cletus was already on the road to the farmhouse beyond.

When the younger man awoke about two hours later, he looked up at Cletus, who was holding a bulky parcel in one hand and a can of cold coffee in the other.

"Breakfast is served!" he announced.

With his well-honed tramp skills, Cletus collected enough dead brush to make a fire, and with a three-stick tripod, heated the coffee and divided the generous portion of breakfast food the kind lady had given them.

Sitting back with a full belly, Cletus expressed his gratitude for the stranger's recommendation.

"That sure was a mighty nice old gal you directed me to," he said, finishing the last crumb of the delicious cornbread from the paper spread before him on the ground.

"She had such a kind and pleasant nature, that one. When I showed up at her door, she treated me just like you said she would--like a human being. I was so surprised at being greeted that way that I didn't know what to say and offered to chop some wood or do any other chore she needed doing to pay for the grub."

Cletus grinned, showing his mouth of crooked, yellow teeth.

"And what do you suppose she said? She smiled a little and said she never did any work herself in the heat of the day and didn't expect to see others do it. She told me to sit in the cool shade of the front porch while she fixed up something for breakfast.

"She went inside and didn't seem the least bit concerned that I'd swipe any of the stuff on the front porch and take off with it."

Cletus watched as the younger man straightened up from where he had been lying on the ground and looked intently towards the little white farmhouse from which Cletus had just returned.

"How did the woman look? he asked, "Did she seem well and happy or strike you as worried and anxious?"

"I dunno," Cletus replied, "I was glad she didn't send me away when she came to the front door. But the way she made me feel was kinda strange. It made me think of churches and Sunday schools and bein' good and all that sort of nonsense that I hadn't thought of since I was a kid. And she didn't look at me like some smelly, dirty bum. No siree. She looked at me with her clear, kind, pleasant eyes. People don't care for folks who look like me, and I was pretty uncomfortable.

A Generous Handout

I'm grateful, and all that, but I got to tell ya, as I came back down here, it got me to thinkin' about what kind of guy I'd have been if I'd had a mother like her. Would the road keep a-calling me as it does now, or would I have been the sort of son she needn't be ashamed to own, with hands clean enough to touch her kind ones?"

"Cut that out, you blithering idiot!" The younger man blurted out angrily. He sprang to his feet, facing Cletus with a livid look on his face and wide blazing eyes. That caught Cletus off guard and the older man stood, eyeing him with wide-mouthed astonishment.

For an instant, the two men faced each other. Then the younger man sank down to the ground with a painful groan.

"Don't mind me, friend," he said hoarsely, "I am not well, and somehow what you said just got on my nerves. I hurt my leg a few days ago, and the pain is killing me."

"Huh!" grunted Cletus, now highly confused and offended; with no other words, the two men stretched themselves out under the shade of the trees to rest until the heat of the day had passed.

Cletus woke a couple of hours later and noticed the other man was in a deep but not restful sleep, tossing and turning with painful moans. He watched him for a while, then dug into the pocket of his blue jeans and picked up a piece of paper that he had taken off a tree on his way back to the farmhouse. He liked to read up on things when things got boring.

When he unfolded the paper, he read:

One Hundred Dollars Reward! We will pay the above amount to any individual for information leading to the arrest and conviction of Jimmy Johnson, wanted for armed robbery.

Description: Age about thirty-two, height about five feet ten inches, weight one hundred fifty-five pounds, complexion fair, eyes brown, hair brown. He has a slight mustache and a curious V-shaped scar on his forehead, just at the edge of his hair. He was shot in the leg while he and his accomplices attempted to hold up a Norfolk & Western mail train on July 15th.

Cletus couldn't believe what he was reading.

"A hundred-dollar reward," he muttered.

The largest sum he had ever possessed was when he stole five dollars.

His wild cloudburst of ideas and images was interrupted as the younger man lying on the ground moaned and moved restlessly.

Cletus glanced at him carelessly and leaned nearer, staring intently, needing to determine if this was the man on the poster. The man's hat had fallen from his head, and there, at the edge of his brown, wavy hair, was a rigid, V-shaped scar, in plain sight. Slowly and deliberately, Cletus again read and compared the description on the paper with the features of the semi-conscious man until it satisfied him that the identity was correct beyond doubt.

Then a wolfish grin exposed his ugly teeth, and he started gloating over his discovery, like a spider spinning its web around its helpless victim.

One hundred dollars!

And all he had to do to claim his reward was to walk down the tracks into town. Cletus figured it would be half an hour's walk to reach the Sheriff and another thirty minutes to come back. Even if the fellow should wake up, he wouldn't get very far in his condition.

The more he thought about it, the more gleeful he became by the moment. Why, it was just like money lying there on the ground. Easy money.

The elated tramp imagined that he could already feel the hundred-dollar bill in his pocket. But as his pockets had big holes, he realized that the bill could fall through the hole onto the ground. No, that wouldn't do at all.

He realized that he would have to get needles and thread to sew up those holes and make his pockets secure.

His thoughts ran ahead of him:

"Needles and thread? Wait!' he mused, "Why not get a new suit and new shoes that didn't have holes in them?"

Cletus immediately saw how far that reward could go.

In 1900, a well-dressed gentleman could get a tailored suit, new shoes, and a fine felt hat for under ten dollars.

And then he stopped and thought: "With a hundred dollars, I could actually buy a ticket and ride inside a train for once instead of clinging to the underside of a freight car. Why, I could even go into a Pullman car and make one of those porters who I only see through the windows, come and wait on me!"

It was as if he had just found "Aladdin's lamp"!

His imagination ran wild. He chuckled as he pictured himself lolling back in the smoking room of a plush Pullman car, ordering the porter about as he had seen other men do. He could go to a hotel and play the gentleman; lounging around and trying his luck with the cards, while the money lasted; even buy drinks for the ladies and maybe have a fling.

Well, what did he care? Easy come…easy go! When the money ran out, there was always the road again.

Cletus stood erect, feeling very much the aristocrat when he became aware that the younger man had awakened and was staring up at him. Seeing the young man as his ticket to new-found wealth, Cletus grunted and spat out viciously, "The jig's up, Johnson. I found one of the wanted posters they're putting up all over town. I didn't know I was in the presence of such a dignitary. You're an easy hundred dollars in my pocket."

"So, are you going to give me up?" asked Johnson.

The way he asked seemed strange to Cletus; there was no anxiety or anger in his voice; just a tired, indifferent tone, as though the answer was of no importance.

"Well, I can't run away, so you needn't be in such a hurry," Johnson said.

The tramp looked at him suspiciously.

"Gifts like you come around once in a life-time," he said,

"I don't get no chance at one hundred dollars every day. And the best thing is, I get this money honest. I don't have to sneak around to get it or run from anybody to keep it."

Cletus hesitated, shifted his feet, and sat down, shaking his head, scowling and muttering to himself.

"I don't see why I should hold back for you. I never seen you until today and it won't do no good to try any tricks on me. I want that money and you bet your sweet life I'm going to have it! You ain't got no strings on me."

The pained look on Johnson's face showed that he was getting frustrated.

"Are you deaf?" the wanted man said, "Didn't I tell you I would be here when you come back? I promise you I won't move a foot from this spot until you get back with the law. Isn't that enough? I'll be glad to end it all. I'm sick and tired of running and hiding."

"It's not that I want to see you pinched," Cletus said apologetically, "I got no beef with you, it's just the money I want."

"Oh yes, the money!" The robber bitterly cried out. "It's always the same with all of us, no matter what or where we are. Money, money! As we stand at the Pearly Gates, I wonder whether Saint Peter will hold out his hand for the required fee."

Cletus stared long and hard at the robber, who lay shaken and white and obviously in great pain with his drawn face gazing up at the fleecy clouds, drifting overhead across the sky. Then, suddenly, the robber flipped himself over, turning face down upon the ground, and sobbed violently.

This surprised Cletus. What was going on with this fella? Feeling most uncomfortable at that moment, the tramp walked away a short distance, then turned and came back.

Laying his rough and dirty hand on Johnson's shoulder, Cletus tried to explain.

"Look," he said, "I'm not an educated person. But it takes no genius to see that what I've said opens a festering wound. Care to tell me your trouble?"

After a couple of minutes Johnson regained his composure. He turned back over and turned his reddened face toward Cletus.

Reaching alongside his body, he picked up a

handful of pebbles and started throwing them at a flock of small sparrows on the ground nearby.

He looked over at the tramp.

"I'll bet you're thinking I'm nothing but a pitiful coward who has reached the end of his rope, aren't you, friend?

"But, you see, it isn't that. I have felt for a long time that it must come down to this moment. I knew that someday I would have to pay the penalty for a wicked, misspent life.

"There was a man I knew who I suspect is now serving a life sentence in prison for crimes that always were about money. When I met him, he didn't seem so bad. I met him on the road, just like I met you today. We were both fugitives just like I am today. He understood my situation because we were both in the same criminal business.

"He gave me a piece of advice; 'Go home, boy,' he said to me. 'Go home and be the man God intended you to be. You may flourish in this trade for a while but vice and sin don't pay, boy, neither in this world nor the next.'

"I was younger then, had just gotten into the business, and I laughed at him. I hadn't yet come to the place where my heart and soul would cry out in loathing at the thing I have now become.

"Look at the despicable creature I've become today. I'm an outcast, a fugitive in the eyes of honest men, spending my days hiding from the law and skulking in the bushes like a hunted animal. Then when it gets dark, I go out and work with others of my kind, robbing houses and businesses. And after we divide the spoils of our scams and robberies, when my accomplices go their separate ways, I sit alone the next day, sinking deeper each day in a hideous swamp of despair.

"You ask me for my story, friend; there isn't much to tell -- it is a common enough one.

"But you, friend, strike me as different. You've somehow managed to exist and stay out of a life of crime. Mine is just the story of one more weak fool without the moral strength to resist temptation when it came knocking. And once I started on that road, Oh, God, how easy it was to keep on sliding!

"I wasn't always this way, you know. I was born on a farm, the only son of a couple of simple, honest parents whose only faults, as best as I can remember, were pampering and humoring me in every one of my selfish, wayward wishes. My father never had the chance of an education and from the day I was born until I was old enough to send off to school, his entire purpose seemed to be educating me so that I could make something of myself.

"My father's dream was to lift me out of the drudgery and hard work of farming. He knew how much I despised it, but it was the only thing he had ever known. He wanted to give me a chance to use my brain and do something with my life, to have a chance at a more successful life than had been possible for him. He wanted me to have the opportunities that were always out of his grasp.

"Well, I got my chance and missed it. I wasted and squandered it. I've wrecked my life and paid the price for my selfishness and ingratitude for the gifts my folks had given me. I was blind and couldn't see my father and mother's lifelong devotion and the sacrifices they made for me. Instead of taking a path they had prepared for me, I've become a failure, a misfit in society, a disgrace to respectable society and a now I am seen as a menace to humankind."

The two men waited in the bushes silently as a long coal train came lumbering by, drowning out their conversation. When it was quiet, Johnson continued, this time with a noticeably softer note in his voice.

"I had a dream a few nights ago, after I got this," touching his wounded leg.

"I had fallen asleep in a big barn where I had been running and hiding from the cops for a couple of days after a heist. In my dream, I was a boy again, and it put me at home in my own warm bed upstairs, looking out my small bedroom window into the branches of the big maple tree outside.

"It was a cool, windy night, and the branches swayed back and forth in the breeze. I could hear them scratching against the side of the house. Then I looked up, and next to my bed appeared a gentle white female figure, her warm hand brushing against my cheek and then she tucked the edge of the warm handmade quilt up under my chin.

"It was then that I recognized my mother's voice, whispering, 'I thought you might be cold, son.'

"Then the sound of the shrill whistle of a passing locomotive off in the distance woke me up. There I was, sleeping in the hay in the barn. Suddenly I was no longer in my dream and a living, waking nightmare replaced those warm, beautiful images. The happy, innocent boy I had been moments before was replaced by a tormented man who was alone, cold, wounded, hunted by the law, and bearing a load of guilt so heavy that I cried out in fear and misery.

"If I were to be honest with you, friend, I have been haunted by a feverish desire to crawl back to my mother's door, to beg her forgiveness for all the heartache I have given her and then lay down and die in peace, resting in that little bed under that warm quilt in my upstairs boyhood bedroom.

"I so yearn to get back home. But today I cannot go back there. I'm now a hunted man with a price on my head and cannot show myself in public, so I must hide each day in these bushes. Even the barns and haylofts are no longer a safe haven for me, as they're looking for me there, too!

With a long-drawn breath, he continued, "There is nothing left for me to do now. I might as well give up. Life in a cell cannot be much more of a hell than mine has been lately. Go on into town and collect that reward. Someone will get it, and you might as well be the one.

"The truth is, you have spoken the first kind words I have heard in a long time. This is the only way I can show that I appreciate it. I will wait here until you get back, or if you want me to, I will try to go in with you. I am feeling better now. The rest has done me some good.

"What are you waiting for? Go on! Time's a-wasting. You'll find me here when you get back. Can't you see I'm about done for? In my condition, I couldn't run to save my own life! Look at me!"

And with that, he pulled up his pant leg, showing his badly swollen leg and a hastily-stitched gunshot wound that had now become infected.

Cletus did not answer at once. He just shook his head. He seemed to be pondering something.

And then he spoke in a quiet voice, saying, "You talk like you'd got close to home today, boss. Do you mind tellin' me if it's hereabouts where your folks live?"

Johnson coughed and shook his head. "My father died some years ago. My mother--" the words came with difficulty--"she was the one who gave you our breakfast today. It was her kind face and the good treatment that you said reminded you of all things that made you feel good.

"As much as I want to go up to her, I could never re-pay her loving kindness by having her see me seeing me dragged off to prison before her eyes. And let's admit it, with those posters everywhere, my capture will happen, sooner or later.

"And, to tell you the truth, my name is not really Johnson. That was one I chose years ago, when I began my new life of crime. I've intentionally changed my appearance over the years since I left home. It is much better that my mother would hear of a Jimmy Johnson being arrested and jailed. The name and image will mean nothing to her. She'll think I'm just another dangerous fugitive that has been brought to justice.

"No, she must never know how close her vagabond son has been to her today."

Cletus sat listening attentively, his eyes focused on the tormented man lying on the ground beside him.

Johnson's sincere witness compelled Cletus to tell his own story.

"Unlike you friend," he began, "I never had nothin' all my life; no fine chances, no home. From the first, I was nothin' but a scrubby little street urchin that nobody wanted. There wasn't ever anyone to care whether I lived or died, let alone live a straight or crooked life.

"So I jest took the easiest way and drifted, eventually ending up in the Army, fighting the war. That's where I got good at livin' off the land. But I can't help wonderin' what would have happened to me if things had been different and I'd a-been born in your shoes. Would I a-went the same way you have? You know, I ain't judging you. Lordy, no! A poor old tramp like me ain't got no right to do that."

Slowly, Cletus rose to his feet, picking up his tattered old hat. As he did so, he said, "Well, I'll be heading out now. I 'spect there's a boxcar waitin' in the freight yard for me. I might have wanted that hundred dollars mighty bad but I can't get it if I don't know where you are. See what I mean?"

Johnson raised himself on one elbow and stared in disbelief at the tramp.

Cletus turned to face Johnson and said, "But before I go, understand one thing, will ya? It ain't for you I'm lettin' all that dough slip through my fingers. I ain't much stuck on the way you've done things. Seems to me you've made a hell of a mess of your life but I guess you're thinkin' that ain't none o' my business.

"I'm walkin' away from you because you're lucky enough to be the son of that kind old lady up on that hill. It'd take more than some reward money to give me a hand in any game that might break her heart or bring tears to those sweet old eyes. Ya understand?

"And y'know the worst part? Goin' up to that farmhouse today got me thinkin' about what kind of son I coulda become if I'd had a mother like the one you've got."

Then Cletus picked up his traveling bundle

and bent forward, and helping Johnson to his feet.

"Look here, buddy," Cletus said, "as much as you be wantin' to, don't you dare go sneakin' round home jest yet; you're still a wanted man in these parts. Lord knows, she's better off without your company and from what you've told me, you've already given her enough hurt and pain to last her a lifetime. Don'tcha think it's better she remembers that boy who was full of promise than the ugly character you've become?

"Stop torturing yerself," Cletus continued, "I suggest you get healed up and stop feeling sorry for yerself. Keep on travelin' and be ready to take whatever's comin' to you, like a man."

"Y'know, if you get far enough away from these parts, you've still got a slim chance of getting away from them that's huntin' for ya. If ya feel em' getting close, give 'em the slip.

"Become a new man. You can start all over again. And if you play it straight, maybe someday you can come back to that sweet woman with clean hands, and not a wanted fugitive. Time has a short memory. The law will stop lookin' for ya in a few years, figuring you've found justice at the end of a rope somewhere else. Will you at least give it a try?"

The warmth of the afternoon sun was now dipping behind the distant hilltop and its last rays shone on the pale, anguished face of Johnson as he stepped close to Cletus and reached out his hand in friendship.

"I promise you," he said slowly, with twitching lips, "I will try, with God as my witness, I will try!"

Slowly the big fingers of the tramp closed over Johnson's hand, and then, without further words, each man turned and started off on in different directions, on their own endless journey. The shiny ribbons of steel rails stretched out off in the distance and then converged and melted into the fading horizon.

As the heavens looked down, the two wanderers appeared like two tiny ants, crawling slowly forward on each of their lonely journeys, toward unknown destinations, somewhere further down the line.

A TERRIBLE TRAIN ROBBER

IT WAS a most unusual funeral. The newspaper article described a criminal who had died after an unsuccessful breakout from prison. He had spent twenty-nine years and seven months of his life behind bars—and ended up a penniless pauper.

Yet the community where he died had turned out in abundant numbers to pay their respects to the deceased. Mourners lined both sides of the road leading to Memorial Hill Cemetery, watching the ornate funeral carriage pulled by a pair of handsome mares.

The prison where he had been incarcerated had intended to donate the body for a scientific experiment; however, the local mortician retrieved the body and prepared it for burial in a first-rate casket. They provided a funeral plot in the Memorial Hill Cemetery in Milledgeville, Georgia. The deceased's quiet resting place is next to the remains of Georgia governors, legislators, and Civil War soldiers.

How is it that career criminals seem to enjoy more popularity than one would think they deserve?

To understand this level of respect and admiration, one must go back to how he created an identity that was quite unusual for the bandits of his day. And distinguished him from other well-known robbers like Jesse James or Billy the Kid.

He had become known to the public in the U.S. and Canada as the "Gentlemen Robber", a term of endearment given by the media and his followers, but a term despised by law enforcement.

His popularity was not for his brutality but for his acts of kindness. Despite committing several train robberies and escaping from numerous jails and prisons throughout his lawless career, many saw him as a generous folk hero who targeted only exploitative corporations.

What was it about this guy? A "fan club" for a notorious criminal who had spent more than half his adult life in jail?

His name was Bill Miner, although he traveled under several alias names.

He was born Ezra Allen Miner in Vevay Township, near Onondaga, Ingham County, Michigan on December 27, 1846, and was the third child born to Joseph and Harriet Miner. But life on the Michigan frontier was solitary and difficult and Ezra's father died when the boy was ten years old. Shortly thereafter his mother moved the family to California to begin a new life "out west." That's when Ezra decided to live the "Wild West" lifestyle, starting with taking on the more western name "Bill" Miner, to go with his newly- chosen identity.

Bill was educated and loved reading and writing poetry. The works of his hero, Mark Twain, inspired him. He believed Twain's "Jumping

Frog" story was confirmation that he could use his steadily- improving horsemanship and marksmanship in 'jumping' stage coaches in Calaveras County.

The problem was, it turned out that his impression of his own skills and abilities was over-rated. You see, he wasn't all that good at robbing stages and kept getting arrested.

His first conviction for stagecoach robbery was in 1866 when he was just nineteen years old, landing him in a jail cell in San Joaquin County, California.

But Bill (or Billy, as he was sometimes called) would not let jail slow him down. After he got out, he went back to his exploits and got arrested for other stagecoach robberies. His terms in the jails in Placer and Calaveras Counties, California, throughout the 1870's would have seemed to be enough, and a lesser man would have given up.

But that was hardly the case. Young Bill got a great thrill from robbing stagecoaches and was gaining quite a unique reputation.

He had developed a very unusual style. This unorthodox method of robbery was gaining him much respect with victims and observers, almost as much as his increased notoriety with law enforcement.

Victims and coach drivers reported that when Miner held up a stagecoach, he showed a courteous and respectful demeanor to his victims.

He was an excellent marksman but unlike other stagecoach robbers of the day, he never killed anyone. In fact, he instructed his gang of associates not to shoot anyone during their robberies. It was okay to fire their guns as a warning signal if they were being pursued or in threat of capture but never were they to shoot at their robbery victims or law enforcement.

He was also known for the special respect he showed to the ladies traveling in the coaches he robbed. Upon entering a stagecoach, he refused to take the belongings of the women passengers. He had no problem taking the money, guns, watches, and other valuables of the men. But when the fearful ladies offered up their pocketbooks and jewelry, he politely declined to take them.

Each of his robbery victims described a consistent pattern of behavior. He would first enter the coach and yell: "Hands-up," which enabled him and his crew to complete the robbery without getting shot.

No one got shot and they invited the passengers to go along their way. Unlike his contemporaries, he never killed a man and never fired his gun, except in self-defense. He claimed he robbed the rich to help the poor and identified himself as the Robin Hood of the day.

Stagecoach Robbery

His bizarre robbery style had become widely

publicized and readers spread his fame by word of mouth. In fact, he was becoming as well-known as Jesse James. It seems he developed a base of "fans" (both male and female) who appeared to admire the unusual way he went about his business. Thus, his reputation as "the Gentleman Robber" was established.

A rugged and handsome figure, the ladies admired the handsome robber who they reported as being polite and kind to them. Even the male victims quietly admired his daring technique, not to mention their appreciation for his no-shooting policy which distinguished him from other robbers of the day.

His victims consistently and frequently reported his impeccable manners. Years later, his train robbery victims described him as behaving in a similar way.

By 1880, after serving a jail term for his most recent robbery attempt, he was released from prison for good behavior, He seems to have had a charm with jailers and judges even back then.

Miner partnered with a former colleague named Bill Leroy, and the two tried to rob another stagecoach. Apparently, his time in jail hadn't improved his robbery technique. Leroy was caught and lynched but Miner escaped arrest.

Undaunted, he returned to his chosen trade and was arrested by authorities one year later for another stagecoach robbery in Tuolumne County, California. This time, Bill Miner, now branded as a repeat offender, was given a twenty-year sentence to be served at San Quentin. Released two decades later from this prison in 1901, Miner, now age fifty-four, was once again a free man.

During his incarceration, he would receive letters, books and baked goods from women who appreciated the special treatment he had given his robbery victims.

During his captivity, his robbery exploits continued to be publicized, increasing his appeal to fans, many of whom had only read about his exploits.

After his release from San Quentin in 1901, he

went to see his two sisters up in Oregon when, as luck would have it, he ran into Gay Hartman (a former cellmate from San Quentin) and another robber who, like Miner, seemed to get arrested a lot.

Looking back over their past exploits, the two discussed how robbing stagecoaches was a thing of the past. They decided the real money was now to be had in robbing trains. Miner had a thing about how the corporations were victimizing the poor and justified his crimes as a way if stealing back the wealth that these corporations had taken from those less fortunate.

The trains that had replaced stagecoaches now carried the large payrolls and shipments of gold and silver. It certainly sounded like a good target.

But stopping a train involved a very different strategy than a stagecoach, as they discovered the hard way.

It was September 1903 when Bill and two confederates tried to hold up the eastbound Oregon Railroad & Navigation Company passenger train near Portland, Oregon. It was Miner's first attempt at train robbery, and it failed miserably. He and his associates were captured.

Miner, a well-known career criminal, was given a life sentence in an Oregon penitentiary. But, as he had done several times before, he managed to escape that Oregon jail.

Things were getting hot in the States. Wanted posters with Bill Miner's face were being put up all over the west coast. The U.S. authorities had put a bounty of ten thousand dollars on his head. Not wishing to press his luck, he escaped from the U.S. authorities and the Pinkerton Detectives and holed up in a small cabin in Haney, British Columbia.

Train Robbery

Miner was an intelligent fellow who always tried to learn from his past experiences. He studied the method of train robbery that had been used by other infamous bandits such as the Butch Cassidy and The Wild Bunch.

For his next attempt, Miner and his crew would board a train at an isolated location where it had to stop or slow down and then they would commandeer the engine.

They would uncouple the express car that was known to carry the shipments of gold, currency, and mail and then force the engineer to drive the front of the train a few miles further down the track.

He and his accomplices would then plunder the express car, blasting the door open with dynamite if the crewmen inside the car were uncooperative.

Miner's second train holdup, occurring near Mission, British Columbia in 1904, proved more successful with his gang bagging one thousand dollars in cash, six thousand dollars in gold dust and three hundred thousand dollars in negotiable bonds and securities. This holdup was publicized far and wide as the first successful train robbery in Canadian history.

Encouraged by the success of this Canadian heist, a year later Miner went back across the U.S. border and was identified as a suspect in a robbery of a Great Northern Railway passenger train north of Seattle, but he never was apprehended or charged with the crime.

Not wanting to press his luck with the American authorities, who were on the look-out for him, Miner went back across the Canadian border to British Columbia in 1906 and attempted a second train robbery.

This attempt was a colossal flop. Miner had made elaborate escape preparations but these didn't work out.

Needing to re-group, Bill sought to disappear into the local community. Miner had gained a lot of experience blending in and had endeared himself to the people of the local community where he was hiding out in plain sight.

He had established himself as a prospector who worked as a cobbler under the new assumed name of George Edwards. He had learned the cobbler trade while in San Quentin and, having lived as a poor man himself, he offered to mend the shoes of poor children in town. But he refused to repair the shoes of those he felt were "people of means" and were able to pay.

In this disguise, "George" had no trouble making friends. He was quite a charming man. He played the fiddle and showed townspeople how to dance. He became known as a proper gentleman. Nobody in the community ever suspected he could be a bandit. His polite and considerate demeanor and folksy nature appealed to the townspeople.

Although respected in town as a kind and charitable individual, in reality he really hadn't reformed.

As things heated up, the posse hunting him found him in the wilderness where he tried to convince the posse that he was just George Edwards, a simple prospector. His ruse as George Edward fell apart, however. The Pinkerton detectives in Washington and Oregon, who had been hunting him for many years, had alerted the posse to check for a distinctive identifying mark. They were told to look for a tattoo of a "dancing-girl" on Miner's arm, as well as a scar on his hand, and described his eyes as "unmistakable."

So when the posse encountered "George" they turned back Edwards' shirt cuff and found the tattoo of a dancing girl. There it was. The searchers had indeed captured the notorious Bill Miner.

He and his cohorts were convicted of robbery, and "Old Bill" was sent to the British Columbia Penitentiary at New Westminster.

By now, Bill had developed a healthy dislike for incarceration and had learned a thing or two about how to escape from captivity.

While jailed in New Westminster, Bill apparently "got religion" and successfully convinced prison authorities (and the Warden's daughter) to allow him to receive religious books from outside sources. Because Miner was so well-behaved and easy-going, it never dawned on those in charge that he was preparing for an escape, so the books weren't searched. But inside those "good books" was money--lots of money, from his fans.

This lax oversight of the prison staff and Bill's cunning enabled him to escape sixteen months into his sentence, with plenty of inside and outside help.

Miner's escape from New Westminster was as daring and successful as the several criminal exploits that mark his history. He had seized the opportunity seeing how the penitentiary staff was short-handed and when, feigning a sickness, he was being allowed outdoor exercise instead of the being held in close confinement usually accorded life-term criminals.

He masterfully took these things into consideration as he conceived and carried out as bold a plan for escape as had ever been attempted.

In fact, the locals recognizing his "Robin Hood" values felt that despite his criminal acts, he was a person with admirable qualities.

Miner - Wanted Poster

Following his escape from New Westminster,

he crossed back into the United States, setting his sights on Georgia.

His next and final train robbery was in White Sulphur Springs, Georgia, in February 1911. It was considered the first train robbery to have been pulled off in Georgia.

It began with the night telegrapher at the White Sulphur Springs, Georgia, station. Robbers broke into the station and bound him up.

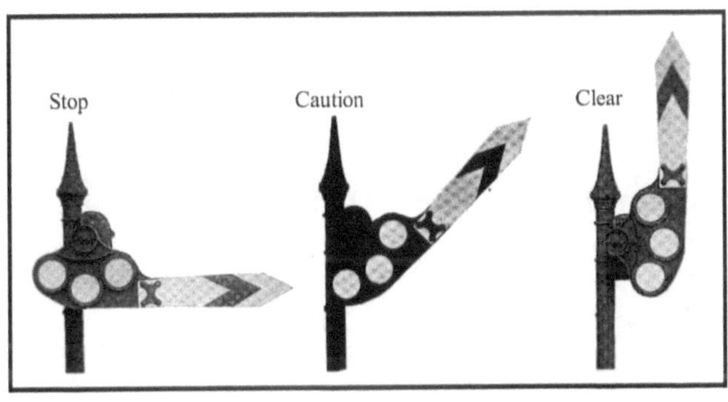

Railroad Semaphore Positions

The seven masked men then proceeded to set the station semaphore signal on the position Stop, ensuring that the incoming Southern Railway No. 36 mail train would come to a halt.

As the engineer stopped the train, the robbers boarded it and forced the engineer at gunpoint to pull the train down the tracks some distance. There, they robbed the express car. They hurt no one in this robbery and the robbers only got a few hundred dollars in cash. However, they failed to open a large safe, which contained a payroll of about sixty-five thousand dollars. The local sheriff organized a posse and after five days, the posse got a lead, which led them to some farms near Dahlonega, Georgia. One farmer they spoke to said there was an old traveler and his two sons had been found sleeping in the loft of his barn.

When the authorities arrived, the barn was empty but Miner was found asleep in a boxcar in a nearby rail yard, with the cash he had stolen lying next to him. Miner identified himself to the Sheriff under the assumed name of George Anderson of Virginia. But, based upon a tip that a Pinkerton detective had provided, they verified they were face-to-face with the notorious robber, Bill Miner. The tattoo of the "dancing girl" had given him away again.

He was cold, hungry, worn out, and didn't offer any resistance.

When Canadian authorities heard about his arrest, they requested that Miner be returned to Canada, where he had escaped previously from prison, and be allowed to complete his life sentence in Canada's New Westminster prison. The local magistrate declined this request.

Miner was tried and sentenced to twenty years in the Georgia State Prison Farm in Milledgeville, Georgia. As the judge pronounced the sentence, the old bandit asked the judge if they could return him to British Columbia to finish his term there. The judge couldn't believe what he was hearing. Miner told the judge his reasoning.

"I never was so well-treated in my life, and I've been in a lot of prisons."

The judge was not amused and sent him straight off to Milledgeville to serve his sentence.

Despite his advanced age, "Old Bill" was still skillful at jail breaks, and in late 1911, he escaped from the prison at Milledgeville. After his first escape, he was re-captured and promptly returned to prison.

His next and final escape attempt was in 1913. For Bill, now 66 years old, this escape would be his last.

Several days after his escape, with the authorities and bloodhounds hot on his trail, they found him hiding in a swamp about twenty miles south of the prison in Toomsboro, Georgia.

When he was discovered, he was tired, sick, and hungry. A boat he had stolen in his escape had capsized, and when it did, he had swallowed some brackish swamp water. The dirty swamp water did him in. Within days of his re-capture, he died in prison of gastritis and intestinal problems.

The Georgia state prison officials could not locate any of Bill's relatives at the time of his death and they ear-marked his body for medical experiments. But when word of this got out, a local Milledgeville mortician named Joseph Alfred Moore stepped forward and requested the body.

Mr. Joe, as the inmates called him, taught Sunday school at the prison and he had become impressed with Miner. Unlike the other hardened criminals he ministered to at Milledgeville, he saw a gentlemanly side in Bill Miner that made him stand out against the others in the general population.

So Mr. Joe purchased a casket and arranged for a burial plot in the Memory Hill Cemetery, where respected and influential residents of Milledgeville were interred. Other local citizens stepped forward, aware of Miner's reputation, and provided donations to pay for Miner's burial clothes.

The local Episcopal pastor came forward to deliver the funeral service, after which Mr. Joe's ornate hearse containing the body of Bill Miner made its way down Liberty Street to his final resting place. You would have thought you were watching a procession for a dignitary, not one you'd expect of a penniless criminal. Well-attired pallbearers slowly walked alongside the horse-drawn funeral wagon, followed by a sizable crowd that included several city officials.

How does this make sense, you might ask?

Perhaps it had to do with the polite, gentlemanly way the notorious "Hands up!" bandit treated people. The way Bill Miner's life ended might suggest that people may overlook the things you did, but they will remember how you made them feel.

ALL ABOARD THE MILK TRAIN

IT WAS 6 a.m. on a typical fall day in 1905 when Leroy Smith opened up the small country rail terminal for the day. He moved about his task with the energy and eagerness one would associate with his 34 years of age. His full head of black hair was neatly combed into position, which remained in place despite the chill of the morning breeze in the valley. His freshly-pressed shirt and brown corduroy vest secured the wool tie around his slender neck. Leroy was a striking figure, one that spoke authority, intelligence, and kindness.

He was one of eight children of a respected dairy-farming family that had been in the local community for three generations. Being the eldest son, his parents expected Leroy to take over the operation of the family farm as his father got older.

A family dairy farm depended upon many hands to perform the many daily tasks of keeping a dairy farm running. Leroy was a quick learner and had learned the dairy business from the inside-out.

His father was very proud of him as he showed how knowledgeable and capable he was with all aspects of the production side of a sizable dairy operation.

So you can imagine his parents' disappointment when, upon his graduation from high school, Leroy stated his intention to apply for a job on the railroad.

Sensitive to his parent's disappointment, he pointed out that the farm was still in good hands. His next two youngest brothers were already committed to continue working with their father on the family dairy farm.

Leroy, however, had a plan. Until the mid

1800's, milk had to be consumed the day of production or immediately turned into butter and cheese. Although butter and cheese had longer shelf lives, the lack of refrigeration and the difficulty of shipping dairy products long-distance were major obstacles for dairy farmers wanting to grow their farms and sell their products. Railroads were changing all of that and especially with the introduction of the Milk Train.

The community where Leroy had grown up had many well-run dairy farms. It was unlike many rural communities in that there were sizable herds of cattle specifically bred for dairy production. Neighboring communities had farms, but most of these had grown only corn, and raised hogs and beef cattle.

With the good grades Leroy had achieved in school, the railroad was very eager to hire promising young men like Leroy, and they offered him a clerk's position in the city.

Upon hearing the news of his decision, Leroy's father became bitter and resentful. But as

Leroy bid farewell to his father and began the walk down the road to the nearby train station, he was comforted to know that the two of them had at least agreed to stay in touch.

The disappointment of Leroy's father was understandable. As the eldest son, the tradition in that area was that the father would take extra care to pass along all the knowledge possessed about dairy farming to his heir. It was unspeakable to think that this generational transfer would not occur as planned.

But Leroy had a bigger plan in mind and his decision to leave the family farm was not driven by ego, greed, or the bright lights of the city. He had two younger brothers who also had been brought up in the family dairy business. Both were hardworking and capable. He had something else in mind.

Although he started his railroad career as a lowly railway clerk, Leroy quickly immersed himself in every aspect of the railroad business, and his work was exemplary, resulting in high praise and excellent reviews from his superiors. These led to several faster-than-expected promotions in the ranks of the company.

He had shown not only competence but mastery in telegraphy, handling of train orders, making out waybills, looking after goods forwarded and received, figuring up damages, and keeping the local grain buyers posted on the daily price of wheat and other commodities.

Leroy learned all the details expected of a Station Agent. Among them was properly identifying the condition of all baggage and freight that were being sent or received at the station. This was recorded on a document called a "way bill".

After fifteen years of working in various railroad positions, he bid on a Station Agent position that had opened up in his hometown. And, he won the position.

When Leroy notified his family of his return, his father was filled with joy. His son had come back home.

Over the years, he came to accept that Leroy

wanted more than life on the farm. And while he didn't understand Leroy's plan, he was beaming with pride that his son had attained a responsible position on the railroad.

Leroy, in reality, had never lost his affection for his family, the farming life, or for the families of other dairy farmers in the district. He had always had a plan and was actively working it. His assignment in the city had enabled him to learn a side of the dairy business that neither he nor his family had been exposed to before.

Now, as the new Station Agent, he dove into this new role with great vigor and enthusiasm.

It was clear from the first day back in his hometown that, unlike his predecessor who was content with just doing his railroad duties, Leroy cared deeply about the welfare of the entire community. By his actions, you could tell he was always looking out for the residents and became respected as a resource townsfolk could reach out to. They would come to the station where Leroy would patiently listen to various issues, needs, or ideas. You could usually count on Leroy to offer a sensible suggestion on how such matters could be resolved.

But Leroy never forgot that one of his most important roles as Station Agent was to ensure that the local farmers' raw milk, which was the town's financial backbone, got safely shipped to its destination in the city, where eager consumers awaited its arrival.

In 1905, the U.S. economy seemed quite robust. Cities were expanding, the nation's population was growing, and the western expansion of the United States seemed to have no bounds.

Producing milk and getting it to the market for processing and sale was a huge business, with over six million independent U.S. dairy farmers producing milk for a growing population of over thirty million American consumers. These consumers wanted milk, skim milk, butter, and cheese. This kept the U.S. dairy industry quite busy, meeting increasing demand and a constant resupply of dairy products.

Dairy products were considered among the best and cheapest foods one could buy and were always in demand, especially by the waves of new immigrants coming to America. But since milk has a relatively short shelf life, there were several steps that need to be taken to keep the milk fresh on its journey from the milk cow to the consumers' table.

One of the most important aspects was that the milk must be kept cool at each stage of the process.

In many smaller communities that only had a few dairy farms, and with refrigeration not widely available, the local farmers would sell practically all the milk they produced locally.

Instead of shipping their milk, these farmers would take their product to a nearby creamery where butter and cheese were made.

But Leroy had come from a larger dairy farming district where there were many dairy farms, some of which were quite large. This district produced much more milk than could be sold locally, so most of the local milk produced here went into the city daily for processing and distribution.

Each evening, the dairy farms in this district would ship their milk to milk plants in the city.

These milk plants would process and bottle the milk and produce butter, cheese and other dairy products. Each morning, in the city, a delivery fleet of milk wagon drivers left the milk plants and would begin early-morning deliveries to households throughout the city and outskirts.

Shipping milk from the rural dairy districts into the city had become a major piece of business for the railroads, and many had designated special "milk trains" for this purpose.

People generally only see the movement of trains and can easily overlook the thousands of people in different departments that are necessary for the trains to move. A railroad operation is a complex undertaking, involving a huge number of people doing specific tasks. In 1905, employment in some railroad communities represented as much as twenty to thirty percent of the area's workforce.

In his twelve-year "apprenticeship" in the city, Leroy was exposed to the complexity of the railroad business. He now had a basic understanding of the railroad's legal, engineering, accounting, and traffic departments, and the treasury, real-estate, and transportation departments.

Unlike the individuals in many of these divisions, a Station Agent requires tactful interaction with the public. Besides mastering all the railroad rules and protocols, Leroy had learned how to deal tactfully with all kinds of people.

Although this was a small rural train station, Leroy's role as the Station Agent was interesting and challenging.

In this capacity, he enjoyed the opportunity to interact daily with many people. He looked forward to each day of serving the local farmers, friends and neighbors, other travelers, and working with the train crews and railroad personnel. He greeted each day with his signature smile and saw each morning as a new adventure, glad that no two days were ever alike.

This morning, as the golden sun rose over the rolling hills in the eastern sky, he knew to expect a few moments of peace and quiet, as well as rushed parts of the day, noisy and chaotic. He wouldn't have it any other way.

Today was off to a good start.

The day began before you knew it. The 7:05 a.m. local train was due in three minutes, and here comes Aunt Mary Clark, who had delayed her departure from home to the station until she saw the column of white smoke billowing from the smokestack of the steam engine coming around the bend.

Leroy was tending to another matter in the back of his office when an anxious Aunt Mary arrived at his ticket window. Eager to get Leroy's attention, she tapped her walking stick on the bars of the ticket window to get his attention.

With a scowl on her seventy-one-year-old face, she glared defiantly, rocking back and forth from one foot to the other in front of Leroy's ticket window, until Leroy left his desk and came back to the open window to handle her request.

However, as Aunt Mary was quite hard of hearing, it was difficult for Leroy to communicate with her. This required additional time to help her purchase her ticket. She had an endless list of questions for Leroy, which caused a string of answers.

Leroy glanced up nervously at the Regulator clock hanging on the wall and then to the train's timetable posted on the wall next to his window.

At that very moment, the Agent's telegraph sounder called him.

Trying not to appear distracted, Leroy listened intently to the message header while dealing with Aunt Mary. The telegraph sounder was producing a series of clicks at different intervals as the electromagnet mechanism opened and closed. The message being communicated in these clicks was in Morse code and Leroy's trained ear could tell it was an important one.

Unlike Western Union telegraph operators, a railroad telegrapher not only had to know Morse code, which employs a set of dots, dashes and spaces to represent numbers and letters, but also the railroad "shorthand" used to convey specific kinds of messages unique to railroad operations.

Telegraph Sounder

The message coming in had to do with the safety of the operation of a distant train and a message that Leroy understood he needed to write down and quickly relay down the line. He understood he could not afford to miss a single click of that instrument because the responsibility would be his if the message was not communicated accurately.

All the while, Aunt Mary continued her loud and incessant rambling, and Leroy, attempting to listen to both conversations, politely looked up and nodded as he carefully wrote down the Morse code message he was picking up from the sounder.

Once he had it copied down, he could give his full attention to his irate passenger and finish issuing Aunt Mary her ticket.

With that task finally completed, he wiped his brow with his pocket handkerchief as he watched Aunt Mary shuffle toward the door leading out to the station platform.

He stepped out of his office for a moment and smiled as he watched the Conductor help Aunt Mary get safely aboard. He heard the steam locomotive's shrill whistle as the 7:05 a.m. passenger train pulled away from the station; right on time.

Fred, the Conductor of the train, turned at the top of the vestibule of the passenger coach, and looking toward the station waved to Leroy with a knowing wink of his eye.

"She's your problem now," Leroy mused as he waved back at the stately gentleman.

Leroy had grown to appreciate Fred and how well he seemed to handle all types of travelers. At fifty years of age, Fred was an imposing figure, in his full Prince Albert Conductor's coat, navy Conductor's cap covering his head of silver hair and his silver Hamilton railroad watch and chain showing in his vest pocket. Still, Leroy was pretty sure he wouldn't want Fred's job.

Going back inside the station and returning to his window, he was now beset by a short-tempered, red-faced man who had just gotten off the last train. This unpleasant fellow was insisting on immediate access to his large steamer trunk, even though it had just been unloaded from the last train.

Leroy explained it was likely still on the baggage cart on the platform and he would see that it would be brought around to the front of the terminal shortly.

Unable to stay grumpy, the curt customer softened when confronted by Leroy's customary grace and humor. The red-faced man's face lightened up and he turned away after thanking Leroy with a smile.

Of all his responsibilities, Leroy understood that as a representative of the railroad, he was the face of the company and must always keep his wits about them.

Leroy's was a smaller rural railroad station. The only railroad employees at that location were Leroy and one baggage handler. As a result, Leroy had to wear many hats. He was responsible for ticket sales, checking in freight and milk deliveries, and having to mind the telegraph. The morning train from the city would drop off and pick up the community mailbag, and Leroy also acted as postmaster too.

Leroy's day was hardly what one would consider boring.

Around noon-time, things got a bit quieter at the terminal. Leroy closed his ticket window, sat down at his desk, opened his lunch pail and took in the gentle fall breeze that circulated through the open windows of the depot. He listened as a locomotive entered the station to drop off the two boxcars that would transport this evening's milk shipment. This break in the action gave Leroy time to reflect on the job he enjoyed so much.

Shortly after lunch time, Leroy made preparations for the "milk train" which would transport the local farmers' produced milk into the milk plants of the city for processing and delivery. For many districts like Leroy's, this daily milk shipment was the backbone of the local economy.

The daily shipment began first thing in the morning, when each farm's dairy cows were being milked, starting at five o'clock in the morning. The herd was milked again at five o'clock in the evening. After each milking, the drawn milk was immediately strained into milk cans and put into a springhouse at each farm to keep the milk cool.

Straining was necessary to remove any debris or impurities from the milking process, and immediate cooling was just as important in order to preserve the raw milk's quality.

Cooling Collected Milk

Each evening, the farmers' wagons would deliver the cans of milk produced for that day to the railroad station for shipment.

Shipment of milk had become more complex

in the fifteen years Leroy had worked for the railroad. In the "old days" each farmer would simply deliver their cans of raw milk to the railroad. But the increased volume of milk being shipped by rail had changed how the railroad handled these shipments, including the development of systems for how milk products were accounted for and shipped.

By 1905, there were also many conflicts occurring between milk producers in the country and operators of milk plants in the cities. As more and more gallons of milk were getting shipped by rail, railroads began charging higher freight rates for special services, such as assigning special "milk trains".

These changes, although necessary, involved an additional transportation expense that was seen as putting the dairy farmers' profits at risk. The dairymen came together to form a Dairyman's Association and this collective of dairy farmers now negotiated freight contracts with the railroad companies for shipping their milk.

The Association established a detailed record-keeping system to oversee all steps in the shipment process. This was intended to protect the producing farmers as well as the railroad. Leroy understood that if a milk can in his shipment was lost or damaged while in the railroad's care, the farmer would be compensated at a low "market rate" set by the milk plants, and it held the railroad liable for these payments.

All Station Agents like Leroy, located in the country stations, and others like him in the city who were involved in the milk shipments were required to complete a set of paperwork and follow established controls associated with the milk shipments.

These procedures, instituted from point of shipment to the unloading of the milk at the milk plant, ensured the return and shipment of the steam-sterilized milk cans to the dairyman.

It wasn't just the dairymen that were getting organized. On the receiving end, the milk processors and dealers also combined and formed the "Milk Exchanges," which constantly battled with the Dairyman's Association over the price they would pay producers for the milk.

But this new record-keeping system was necessary to ensure that each farmer was paid accurately and honestly.

As a Station Agent, Leroy had to see that milk tickets accompanied all milk cans offered for shipment by a dairyman. He would then prepare a waybill for each farm's milk, of which he kept a detailed record.

When the milk train arrived, he would hand the milk waybills for this shipment to the Conductor, whose job was to check the waybills, noting any errors. Leroy's waybills were always one hundred percent accurate—he was very good at his job.

Once the milk train arrived at the milk plant in the city, the Conductor would deliver these waybills to another Agent, who then had to secure the consignee's receipt. The Agent promptly sent these two sets of documents to the Ticket Auditor. Once the Ticket Auditor confirmed shipment, the farmer would get paid.

As temperature control continued to be a major factor in the milk plant accepting each farmer's milk, the destination Agent's responsibility also included watching the shipment as it was being unloaded. He watched to ensure that the milk cans from the train did not sit unattended at the terminal of the milk plant, which could compromise the milk quality.

But there had been other changes, at a local level, that had happened in the past few years that concerned Leroy.

Dairy farmers knew how to protect their milk but when the milk was transported from the farm to the railroad terminal, that step of the process exposed risks to the shipments. Being a dairyman himself, Leroy saw what could happen to the milk during transport.

He wasn't as worried about the incoming shipments from the farmers he knew as he was about the commercial drivers recently hired by farmers to bring daily milk deliveries to the stations.

Each day, he greeted the dairy farmers driving up with cans of milk in the back of their wagons. He knew these farmers and their operations personally and was comfortable they had taken all steps to preserve the quality of their product.

But some farms had hired commercial drivers that just didn't sit well with him. Leroy didn't care for these drivers as much. They were just working to collect a paycheck and didn't seem as careful about the cargo they were hauling. He had seen first-hand some of the carelessness and problems these commercial drivers caused.

He had experienced commercial delivery drivers that mixed up the lots of milk picked up at various farms along their route. This created great confusion at the railroad terminal and caused Leroy significant time to straighten things out.

With each delivery of these commercial drivers, Leroy paid attention to the little details and watched their behavior closely. He had caught a dishonest driver on his platform trying to tamper with cans of another farmer's milk. These men, not part of the local community, were just in it for the paycheck and some would stoop to dishonest acts for a bribe of a few dollars. This is the reason a dairy farm rating system was put in place.

In 1904, the Bureau of Animal Industry had announced what was to become an official scorecard of dairy farm inspections intended to promote friendly rivalry among dairymen. The Bureau designed this numerical rating system to tell the community each dairy's standing in relation to producing a sanitary milk supply. Not all dairymen welcomed these inspections, and some tried to damage the rating of their competitors.

And it wasn't just malicious tampering that could harm the milk.

The farm-to-depot stage of milk delivery was fraught with other things that could damage or deteriorate the milk. The commercial drivers were assigned a pick-up route that followed the main road through the community. Farmers using commercial transport services, who lived on farm roads, would bring their milk out to the road after the evening milking, where it would sit on a wooden stand until picked up by the commercial driver.

If the driver became lost or was late with his pickup, that day's milk shipment might miss the night train.

Also, while sitting on the main road awaiting pick-up, these milk cans were exposed to the elements or were readily available to any persons with poor intentions who might seek to destroy the milk or damage its contents.

So he had valid concerns about these deliveries and hence his caution about accepting them without further inspection.

It was now 4:45 p.m. and the last of the day's passenger and freight trains had passed through, leaving only the evening's Milk Train yet to arrive.

Afternoon Milk Delivery

Leroy set about finishing final preparations for the arrival of the farmers' milk wagons for the night milk train. With the platform cleared, Leroy and his baggage handler made way for the day's most important shipment. This train carried the local farmers' milk from Leroy's station and several others into the milk plants of the city for processing.

Depending upon the time of year, Leroy could expect to receive a shipment made up of twenty-quart and forty-quart milk cans. Many dairy farmers felt that the milk from their farms was kept in better condition in the smaller cans, especially in very hot or very cold weather.

The farmers and their drivers arrived at the station shortly after suppertime in wagons loaded with their day's milk production.

Leroy received each milk can and checked it in, keeping each farm's cans together. Then a dry, clean blanket, marked with the shipper's name, was thrown over each farmer's cans, to maintain the temperature of the milk.

Earlier in the afternoon, the station had received two special milk cars that sat on the siding, its own platform connected to the station.

Loading the Days Shipment

Leroy recorded each farmer's shipment, loaded each set of cans into the two milk rail cars, and covered them up. In warmer weather, once loaded, he iced the cans down. It was not fifteen minutes after the car door was closed and sealed before Leroy heard the shrill whistle of the milk train arriving. The train arrived at the depot and the locomotive made a quick switching procedure to pick up the two box cars containing the milk waiting on the special siding that was next to the terminal platform. With no further delay, the train departed the station on schedule.

Further down the line, that same train picked up more milk cars loaded at other stations in the same manner. Finally, where the branch line intersected with the main line, the train was now of considerable size, loaded with twenty-two milk cars, and cleared for a ninety-minute dash into the city. It gave the section dispatcher priority track rights and allowed the milk train to run at top speed. The "precious cargo" of the milk train had to move quickly. "First-day" milk got a top price from the milk plants in the city.

As the milk train departed his station, Leroy smiled, satisfied that this had been a good day. Everything had pretty much gone according to plan, and the local dairy farmers could expect to get a good price for their day's milk.

He ensured that each can of incoming milk was properly accounted for. Once he took it into his care, he knew it was in a safe, secure place until he personally loaded each can into the milk cars.

Before taking the job as a Station Agent, he had grown up as a dairy farmer so he was well aware of the things that would affect the temperature or quality of the milk being shipped.

Leroy understood fully well that temperature control began on the farm. His family, like most of the dairy farms in the district, had a sizable spring house. The milk was drawn here twice a day and rapidly cooled after collection.

This kept the milk cool until it was time to be transported that evening to the railroad. Once cooled, milk sours very quickly when it warms up. A common complaint that Agents heard from the milk processors in the city was milk in cans that contained sour milk.

From time to time, he had to deliver bad news in his role as Station Agent. Leroy might find himself being yelled at by a farmer who had learned that part of his shipment was rejected at the milk plant because it had gone sour. The farmer felt sure he had done everything right. Most times, it was what had happened after the milk had left the farm.

Leroy took these issues personally. He understood he was the dairy farmer's most important quality control checkpoint after leaving his farm. He worked hard and took every step within the scope of his role to ensure their fresh milk was accepted by the milk plant in the city.

Milk transport in the early 20th Century was a tricky thing. That meant everyone involved in the production or shipment of milk knew what was necessary to maintain the proper temperature and keep it in an acceptable range throughout shipping. Fifty-five degrees was low enough, and sixty degrees was thought to do very well as long as the milk was not exposed to unusual risks in its transportation.

Leroy understood the necessity and importance of keeping the milk at just the right temperature. Both summer and winter presented unique challenges to dairymen, and Leroy looked for specific things in the shipments he checked in. In very hot weather, farmers would place a glass jar or bottle filled with pounded ice and hung in the milk cans to keep the milk cool. In cold weather, the cans might arrive in a box lined with woolen, felt, or quilting of wool, and a hot brick in each corner in a sheet iron receptacle to prevent milk freezing.

One reason Leroy was so respected as the Station Agent was that he was the third generation of a local dairy farm and had learned from his father and grandfather that success in the dairy business means everyone has an important job to do. Grazing, feed, and barn sanitation are all prerequisites to cows producing good milk. Leroy had learned all the "tricks of the trade" from his father, how to select the best cattle for his herd and how to fatten them up and get them to the stage where each cow was producing eight to ten quarts a day of heavy, well-flavored and dense milk. But the last step in the "milk to market" process was the most critical - keeping the milk at the correct temperature and keeping the milk pure all the way to the creamery or milk plant.

Because of the way his father had taught him about the dairy business, he knew much more about what it took to get a milk shipment to the city than did any of his Agent counterparts. And it earned him the respect and admiration of the farmers he worked hard each day to serve.

As Leroy prepared to close the depot for the evening, he went over the day's records before storing them away. Record keeping, after all, was an important part of his job.

The day's work done, Leroy shut down the station for the night, pulled out a stick of Dentyne chewing gum, popped it in his mouth, and headed home for the day. A broad smile crossed his face as the weary but happy Leroy reveled in the fact that in his Station Agent role, he was a critical factor in protecting the financial livelihood and future of the entire dairy district he had grown up and loved so much.

I WANT TO MEET THE ENGINEER

THE YEAR was 1946, and a very excited thirteen-year old Paul scrambled up into the cab of the locomotive.

He was absolutely beside himself. Today he was getting his first-ever locomotive cab ride, thanks to his Uncle Buck, who worked as a locomotive fireman on a local passenger train.

Paul, the son of a third-generation southern Illinois farmer, had been taken by railroad life ever since seeing his first train cut across the plains of southern Illinois as a child. His dreams were to someday actually be in the cab of a working locomotive. And today, after several years of pleading, his uncle had made arrangements to get his nephew into the locomotive cab where he could experience railroading first hand.

His uncle, positioned at his station on the left side of the locomotive, looked back and saw his train being overtaken by the sleek California Zephyr passenger train, just leaving the yards of Chicago and quickly drawing alongside Uncle Buck's locomotive, which was pulling thirteen freight cars today.

Uncle Buck cast a glance across to the knowing eyes of the Engineer, who knew what came next. The two men never exchanged a word, but almost instantly and with few motions, he felt the powerful engine he was in start to smoothly pickup speed, thanks to the expert knowledge and mastery the Engineer had of his locomotive.

What happened next was a magical moment being forever etched in young Paul's memory.

With only a slight jolt, Paul felt the train speed up as the Engineer gradually opened up his throttle, seeking to match the speed of the Limited that was about to pass them. Something special was happening.

Did the streamlined locomotive that was pulling the Limited also sense what was happening?

From young Paul's point of view, he knew exactly what was going on. It was a locomotive race. He had heard stories about this, and now he was actually in one!

The expertise and experience of the two locomotive engineers and firemen were being put to the test. Uncle Buck told Paul to stay to the side of the cab as he went to work.

Uncle Buck was a big man, with human arms of steel. Being a fireman on a steam locomotive demanded not only mental agility but incredible stamina and physical strength. On a typical run, he would ordinarily shovel some seventeen tons of coal from the tender attached to the locomotive into the engine's raging firebox.

The doors to the firebox opened and shut with a predictable rhythm as Uncle Buck's coal shovel moved in a swift, smooth fashion from the tender to the engine, with each opening of the firebox clanking with the rhythm of a skilled musician. Paul watched with a great fascination with each firebox opening, seeing with his own eyes what his preacher had told him the fires of hell looked like. The firebox seemed to have an insatiable appetite. The roar and heat blast of each opening of the firebox even felt like the gates of hell opening and closing before his very eyes.

He had never seen his uncle in this way. He was in combat, and his adversary was this insatiable fiery monster demanding to be fed. Uncle Buck was unstoppable, with the movement of a dancer going back and forth from the rocking floor of the swaying tender, then turning with a new shovelful of tender coal and skillfully delivering it to the opening firebox door.

He looked away from this scene for a moment to turn back to the Limited, which was now alongside his train, going approximately the same speed. Some of the Limited's passengers were looking out their wide windows across to Paul's train. He wondered what the passengers on the other train thought of the other at that moment.

Paul observed intently the sleek and shiny luxuriously- appointed heavyweight Pullman cars of the Limited. It was a glimpse of a rich and pampered existence he had never before seen, and it was beyond his comprehension.

Growing up on the family farm, his family had fared better than the typical American. They had been spared some of the austerity that the war had imposed on the nation. Despite the obstacles they faced, American farmers had expanded their crop acreage during the war. And thanks to advances in farming technology, his father had increased their harvested acres of corn, wheat, and oats by a significant amount. They were considered comfortable, but not wealthy.

Here, Paul found himself looking at a slice of society that seemed to have been totally untouched.

Young Paul gazed down into the passing parlor

car that was oozing with its sumptuous appointments and superior comforts and amenities.

Through the windows of that car, he spotted a lovely blond-haired lady that he guessed to be about twenty years old. She looked like a model, sitting lazily in the tufted wingback chair, adorned in a red silk dress; her shapely legs carelessly crossed, and one hand holding an opened magazine in her lap, face down.

Parlor Car

His face blushed as he watched her, certain that she was unaware of the nearby admirer. Yet he was entranced by her beauty and gracefulness. His imagination began to run wild as he watched her. The slender, tapered fingers of her other hand began mindlessly fumbling with a golden locket at the end of a braided chain.

The moment only lasted a few fleeting seconds. And, just like that, the Limited had pulled ahead past them and was now racing off into the distance.

But for young Paul, these images became forever etched in his imagination.

"By golly!" He thought, "There is nothing better than being a train engineer."

Following that experience, each time his Uncle Buck came to visit, the two would continue to talk about railroad life. His uncle had seen the excitement in young Paul and understood his enthusiasm. Sitting on his father's front porch, they would talk about train life for hours on end until the two were called in for Sunday supper.

One afternoon Paul asked, "Uncle Buck, what does it take to become a Locomotive Engineer?"

"Well, Paul, I'm only a fireman and hope someday to become an engineer, but I can tell you it's a long, hard path. I started at the beginning by a meeting my dad, your late grandfather, had set up for me.

"He knew the Road Foreman of Engines who got me a job doing various odd chores, calling crews, wiping engines, and the like, at the big roundhouse. It was hard work, but it was where I first experienced the romance of trains. The roundhouse is a magical place full of fog and engine smoke, often thick enough to cut.

Then I got promoted to a hostler. The 'hostler' and the 'stalls' of the roundhouses go way back to the days of old when horses pulled the carriages along the rails' motive power.

"I got to know the engine crews and there were times, usually odd times at night, where there was an occasional opportunity to ride in the engine cabs as the engines were being moved in and out of the roundhouse. It wasn't as busy as daytime. The engine man operating the locomotive had time to show me each of the items in the cab, and from this I gradually acquired a knowledge of the locomotives that you can't get just from reading a book.

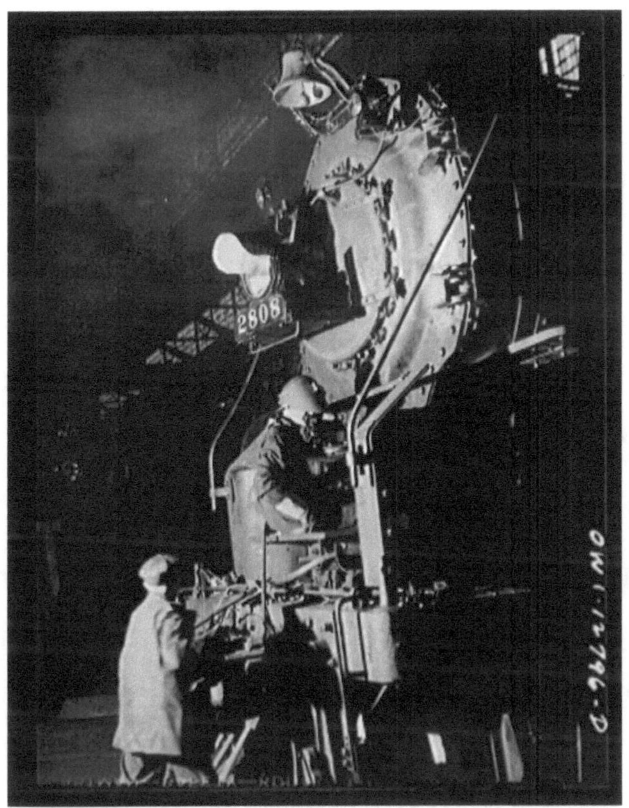

Working on Engine in the Roundhouse

"The Roundhouse is a great place to build your reputation because it shows what you are made of. One day, there was a vacancy on one of the engine crews. The Road Foreman of Engines gave me a good report to the Trainmaster for my work in the Roundhouse. The Trainmaster is the person who handles the train and engine crews, and it was he who promoted me to fireman.

"In that role, I traveled the division end to end, on one train or another, day in and day out. I quickly came to understand why the railroad requires physical, eyesight, and hearing tests to be assigned to a position in a locomotive cab. It is no slight task firing a heavy steam locomotive over a hundred or more miles of grade climbing, curve-rounding railroad.

"The job, as you have seen for yourself, calls for human arms of steel to handle feeding ton after ton of coal into the locomotive's demanding firebox. If I do not stay hard at it there on the rocking floor of the swaying tender, the locomotive will lose power.

"But if you continue to do your job well every day, every run, the day will come when you get to become an engineer. As a fireman, you will get to know the line very well during your countless trips over it. In my case, it enabled me to know every signal, bridge, station, and curve, every grade, every place for slow, careful running, and every place where the train can speed up.

"I know you like to read the works of Mark Twain. I did too! I realized that just like Twain described the work of a riverboat pilot, I had to know my line just as the pilot learns the river by heart every twist, bend, shallow, rapid, or obstruction along its way.

"When you get to be a Fireman, Paul, there are many times you may find you have to assume temporary charge of the engine. So once you get to that level, you have to be qualified to sit in the right hand of the cab, and to take command over the engine's reverse lever and throttle if that becomes necessary."

But since Paul understood that to work for the railroad, one needed to be twenty-one years old, Paul applied himself in school and in 1954, he reached the age for acceptance in the railroad's program to become an engineer. He had met all the minimum entry requirements to begin the Engineer's apprenticeship. His good grades enabled him to get his high school diploma, and he easily passed the tests confirming he had sharp vision and hearing and possessed good hand-eye coordination.

Additionally, in the three years since he had graduated, Paul had also taken Uncle Buck's advice and had gotten a position at the Roundhouse in the city and had learned a great deal there. His uncle was respected, and his recommendation came with high expectations. So Paul applied himself, and when he was approaching his twenty first birthday, the Road Foreman of Engines and Trainmaster also recommended Paul to the company that he be considered for the program where new Engineers got trained.

While working in the Roundhouse, Paul had honed his mechanical skills. He knew railroad engineers needed to be mechanically minded, and when he sat in front of the examiners, did very well on these interviews. He was confident that he had shown the railroad examiners that he not only had knowledge but also had the sound judgment and high levels of physical stamina that the job required.

But in 1954, the job of an Engineer had changed dramatically from a decade before and the position was becoming more competitive. His Engineer apprenticeship now had several additional requirements for him to complete before he could take his Engineers license exam. Becoming an engineer differed from what Uncle Buck had described to him back on the farm.

But Paul recognized that railroad life was evolving, and he patiently worked through each area of his training, continually building up his knowledge and skills. As he had seen working in the Roundhouse, times were indeed changing on the railroad, and the "old school" ways were being reshaped by new technology on the line, as well as in the locomotive cab. Most of the railroads were now using Diesel-electric locomotives, and many were scrapping the steam locomotives of his youth. And each year, he saw new approaches to signaling, communications, and switching.

Paul finally realized his dream as he received his license as a train engineer in 1966. But achieving this important career milestone didn't feel the same as he had hoped. By that time, the heyday of passenger service had passed, except for Amtrak and some regional commuter trains. Instead of wrestling massive steam locomotives, he was now driving diesel locomotives and pulling freight trains. Most of the beloved and colorful railroads he had grown up with had either gone out of business or were consolidated into a nationwide rail service called Conrail, his current employer.

There was an ever-increasing set of rules, guidelines, and restrictions a train crew needed to follow, and constant pressure from the head office to reduce headcount to increase efficiency. This wasn't the way he had envisioned working on the railroad at all. And he sometimes wondered why he had chosen this career years before. These moments made him feel depressed and weary.

In June 1984, Conrail, seeking to reduce head-count, had announced an early retirement program, and Paul, now fifty-one years of age, thought to himself, "Perhaps it's time for me to go." In those moments, he thought of how nice it might be to spend more time with family or pursuing his many hobbies. The paycheck had been steady and nice, but it wasn't giving him the joy he had so anticipated.

The morning of the twelfth of August 1984 started as a normal workday for Paul. His train orders were to take four GP40 diesel locomotives deadheading up to Buffalo from the railyard in Erie, Pennsylvania. After getting the four three thousand horsepower locomotives hooked up together, he and his fireman led his short but powerful train out of the yard into the northbound main line.

A few miles out of the rail yard in Erie, Pennsylvania, he spied a long steam excursion train pulling out of the yards onto an adjacent track. Increasing his locomotive's speed slightly, he caught up with the train and to his amazement found himself looking at a beautiful twenty-two car train made up of restored first class Pullman and coach cars of different vintages. It was being pulled by the legendary streamlined Norfolk & Western 611 steam locomotive.

The 611 was one of the J Class Steam locomotives that had been built in 1950, specifically for high-speed passenger service.

"Is this a dream?"

611 Engine Coming Through

Paul pinched himself. No, this was quite real. He slowed his diesels a bit to match the ambling gait of the 611, hoping to catch the attention of the fireman or engineer.

The 611 was running alongside the Conrail mainline on the "old" Nickel Plate line that still had the thirty-nine-foot rail sections that treated its passengers to the old "clickety-clack" of the rails. Except for lesser traveled routes and sidings, this type of track was being replaced on mainlines by newer, quieter continuous welded rail.

As Paul pulled alongside the sleek steam locomotive, the joy he felt as a thirteen-year-old flooded back into his heart. He smiled as he saw the beautifully restored Pullman cars packed with rail fans with colorful hats and cameras, and sightseers and families with young kids, all looking out the windows, or happily moving about between the cars. The 611 was now starting to pick up speed, and Paul watched it pull gracefully ahead.

Hoping to recapture his childhood experience, Paul's eyes searched each passing Pullman and Coach, wondering if there might be a young blond-haired girl in a red silk dress among them.

Paul slowly increased his engine's speed and edged closer and closer to the front of the excursion train. He was in awe, gazing upon the beauty of this massive steam engine. The locomotive looked to Paul as if it were a crouched panther, ready to pounce on its prey.

As he approached the 611 cab, he cast a wave across to its fireman. The fireman waved back to Paul, and then an unexpected thing happened.

The dignified and stately 611 locomotive suddenly sprung to life, as its fireman opened up the automatic stoker feeding the fire in the boiler, and started turning the valves as the engineer pulled on the throttle and the long heavy passenger train came to life, surging.

Paul smiled and said to his fireman.

"Look at that! The big cat has been awakened!"

As the adjacent train started to pull ahead, Paul recalled that the streamlined 611 locomotive had been specifically built for a one hundred eleven miles per hour mainline passenger service and was more than capable of pulling the kind of long, heavy train she had today. It was, after all, a legendary locomotive, with massive seventy-inch diameter driving wheels, and capable of eighty thousand pounds of tractive effort.

And Paul saw this latest move as an invitation to a locomotive race, like what he had experienced at age thirteen. This was the chance of a lifetime.

Instead of letting the 611 slip away, Paul responded by opening the throttles of his diesels and immediately felt the four interconnected locomotives respond with a loud unanimous roar, and sending a plume of diesel exhaust high into the air.

Inside the excursion train, an attentive Conductor had gotten on the PA system and suggested the passengers look out the left side of their cars. The older cars that had openable side windows went down, and everyone rushed to the side to see the train race that was now appearing to be underway.

The mood inside the Pullman and coaches seemed to be delirious, with the passengers hooting and shouting, "Go-go-go!" As the speed of the 611 increased, Paul tried to match it with the combined power of the four Conrail engines.

And then, sensing that it had something to prove, the excursion train started to steadily pull away. The excited passengers watched the train speed increase by timing the wayside mileposts along the roadbed that flashed by faster and faster. In a matter of a couple of minutes, the straining Conrail locomotives, unable to keep up, disappeared from view at the rear of the excursion train.

A half-hour later, as Paul guided his four locomotives into a siding at the Buffalo yards, the gleaming triumphant 611 stood defiantly, having taken on coal and water for its return trip. The passengers had disembarked and were off the train in the yard taking photographs of the train, the yards, buildings, and the 611 train crew.

Paul recognized this as a once-in-a-lifetime

moment. He parked his engines on a siding and walked over to the crowd. He stepped up to one of those dressed as a Conductor and asked,

"Could you tell me where I could find the engineer at the throttle of the 611? I'd sure like to meet him."

The conductor escorted Paul over to the Engineer and introduced him to the stately figure. Paul, with great excitement and a trembling hand, took the hand of the Engineer and then unexpectedly broke into tears.

Moved by his reaction, the Engineer asked,

"Son, are you okay?"

Paul smiled and said, "I only wish my son were with me today. I so wished I could have shown him first-hand what it was like when they knew how to run a railroad."

In losing this brief race, Paul realized he had won something much greater than he ever imagined: an opportunity to return to his childhood dream of working on the railroad.

LOVE ON A TRAIN

IT WAS two weeks before Christmas 1950, and Curtis sat quietly looking out the frosted window of his modest apartment overlooking the Point in downtown Pittsburgh, flanked by the convergence of the three ice-crusted rivers below.

Unable to sleep, like most nights, he found himself staring across the river at the Pennsylvania Railroad station as the old regulator clock on his wall chimed once, telling him it was now 1:15 a.m.

As he had done so many times before, he watched the "Liberty Limited" passenger train pull into the station below, and the stream of passengers disembark, tonight bundled up against the bitter cold, scurrying across the platform to the warmth of the station doors. A tear ran down his wrinkled cheek and fell to the floor.

Curtis, now seventy-six years old, was a mere shadow of his younger self, but could not shake the events of that fateful night fifty years ago. In the wee hours of the night, he would awake, returning to the recollection of another evening he could not get out of his head.

The young man had boarded the westbound B&O passenger train at Harpers Ferry, West Virginia. It had been a terribly cold day with the temperature dropping, a brisk wind whipping off the Potomac River accompanying the snowfall coming up into the Shenandoah Valley. The skies overhead were threatening; very dark and ominous.

The sleek and powerful black 2-8-0 steam locomotive, with its cargo of five dimly lit passenger cars, slowly pulled away from the station.

The engine began to pick up speed, but even with a raging inferno in the locomotive's firebox, it was already evident that it was straining against the increasing mountainous terrain.

Up in the cab of the locomotive, its crew were embroiled in a life-or-death struggle, not just about getting the locomotive up to speed but also fighting against a demanding train schedule, made challenging in the face of this fierce oncoming winter blizzard. The tall smokestack of the locomotive billowed with huge plumes of white smoke while its eight large steel-driving wheels created showers of sparks as they clawed for traction against the frozen steel rails.

Fighting the Winter Storm

Curtis had boarded the third car of the train into a warm and somewhat stuffy coach car that had several rows of seats facing each other. As most of the seats of the car were already occupied, he found a seat where the only other occupant was a fashionably dressed young woman in her twenties, wearing a large, wide-brimmed hat with two colorful feathers. She cradled a tiny infant in her arms, wrapped in a warm blue blanket.

Curtis awkwardly introduced himself and inquired whether he might take the seat across from her.

The young lady, named Clara looked up at him with a blank stare, examining the young man, thinking,

"One can't be too cautious, after all."

The young man wasn't unattractive and appeared to be similar in age, with a slightly muscular build, and attired in a tailored three-piece herringbone suit and felt derby hat.

Curtis

With a somewhat dismissive wave of her hand, she nodded and muttered, "That's fine with me,"

Curtis awkwardly took the seat opposite that had been offered.

Clara glanced up at him. Her father, a corporate executive in New York, wore the same type of suit. It was a suit that a strong, confident, serious man would wear.

Shortly after the train's departure from Harper's Ferry, Roger, the train conductor, came through the car and validated Curtis's ticket.

He had kept a watchful eye over the woman and her infant for several hours since they had boarded this train in Wilmington, Delaware. Clara had traveled across several states, and the stress and exhaustion of the trip were showing on her pretty face. It had not been a comfortable trip for her, given the annoyance and discomfort of spending the day and night in an overheated, poorly ventilated passenger car. The grimace on Clara's face bore the evidence of the trip's toll.

Curtis remained cautious, since his initial attempts at discussion had failed with the young woman. He wanted to engage in light conversation with the lady, who, at the moment, seemed unhappy.

He thought to himself, "Surely there must be something I can say to cheer this lady up."

What Curtis could not have known was that her troubles were not just because of the physical discomfort of the trip. A significant part of Clara's unrest was magnified by the grief and fear inside this recently-widowed young lady, for tonight she was taking a major step into the unknown.

The small brocaded silk traveling bag she kept by her side contained a handwritten letter of invitation she had recently received from her late husband's elderly aunt and uncle, whom she had never met.

It read: "Please come live with us. We live in a tiny hamlet nestled away in the mountains of Western Pennsylvania. We would like to offer the two of you a safe sanctuary, far away from the city where you suffered your harrowing loss."

Included with that letter of invitation, Clare had received a set of train tickets, accompanied by detailed instructions on which train to take in order to travel to their location.

The remote hamlet where the aunt and uncle lived was what was called on the railroad a Flag Stop. This was not a regular railroad station but simply a rural platform sitting alongside the main line, where the train would only stop if they had instructions for a passenger to get on or be let off.

Curtis considered himself an observer of small but important details. Here he found himself seated across from an attractive woman in stylish attire, who he surmised had come from a good upbringing, perhaps even society. The ornate silver wedding band on her hand told him she was married.

Being a polite gentleman, Curtis felt a bit awkward with his assessment and didn't want to appear forward to this stranger. He simply wanted to try to make the journey they were both on a bit more pleasant.

As the night wore on, he discretely watched Clara as she fell in and out of sleep, which was usually interrupted when the rhythmic clickety-clack of the rails became a loud bang and rocked the car as the train went over a turnout along the main line.

After a couple of hours of awkward exchanges, the two young people had finally managed to strike up a conversation.

It began slowly, with Curtis and Clara, the young mother, sharing information about each of their destinations.

Curtis began and told Clara he was destined for Pittsburgh, Pennsylvania, to take on an important job for the railroad. Clara confided that she and her son were going to spend some time with relatives in Western Pennsylvania.

A few basic pleasantries followed that conversation, commenting on the weather and the stuffiness of the railcar. As the two became more familiar and comfortable with each other, Clara shared details of her circumstance with Curtis and why she was traveling without a husband on this trip.

Curtis shared he was from a small city in Maryland, had completed high school, and worked for the B&O railroad as an extra telegraph operator. He explained that he'd learned the telegraphy craft not by formal education, but by hanging around and learning from the men that worked in the small railroad and telegraph offices near where he lived. He had worked his way up from messenger and clerk jobs to become an extra telegraph operator.

However, in that role, income was unpredictable; the extras were only called upon when the railroad got busy and needed extra hands.

Clara smiled warmly. Clearly, this young man had ambition and was going somewhere. Perhaps getting to know him better would be a good thing.

Throughout the evening, as the train approached each station stop, their conversation was interrupted as Roger, the train conductor, would walk through each car loudly announcing the name of the upcoming station. The next station being announced was Cumberland, Maryland.

Clara was exhausted and was fighting sleep, but it was becoming clear that such rest, with frequent station stops, was not likely to happen on this train. Feeling more physically and emotionally drained with each trip the conductor made through the third car, Clara would reach out and plead with him, "If I doze off, please do not forget me!"

Roger assured her, saying, "No, madam, I'll see that you get off at your stop all right." He would then glance at his Hamilton pocket watch and confirm, "We are still on time and scheduled to reach your destination at ten minutes past three this morning."

Sensitive to her state of anxiety, Curtis boldly reached over, touched her arm lightly, and whispered, "Miss, don't worry, I'll see that you get off at your stop."

The rigid features of her slender face loosened as she heard these words, and her lips relaxed into a small but warm smile.

That moment seemed to take their relationship to a new level. The two young people now exchanged bits about each of their hopes and dreams.

As Curtis suspected, Clara was indeed an educated woman who had been schooled in the arts. She shared her love of the works of William Shakespeare and was particularly fond of his play, "All's Well That Ends Well." In fact, in trying times like tonight, she admitted repeating to herself her favorite line from the play - "Love all, trust a few, do wrong to none."

Curtis confided that he wanted a more secure and better life than was possible back home. In order to obtain a full-time position with the railroad, it would require a move to a different and larger railway office. And while railroad telegraphers' pay was on a par with that of skilled blue-collar workers in the factories, he wanted to be recognized as a professional telegrapher. He understood that this meant a move to the "professional" tier jobs of the railroad. The more casual attire of a messenger would be replaced by suits and ties and shined shoes. He would be expected to live in middle-class housing, eat middle-class meals, and partake of middle-class entertainment.

So while taking and relaying messages across the railroad telegraph, he had learned about the position that was coming available at the large and busy Pittsburgh terminal. He went to his supervisor and told him how badly he wanted this position. He received a glowing reference from his supervisor that was instrumental in him securing the full-time position as an Agent at the railroad's large Pittsburgh district. This was how he came to be on this evening's westbound train.

Curtis asked if he could provide Clara his new address so the two could keep in contact via the mail when he noticed Clara had nodded off to sleep again. The rhythm of the engine and the tracks had lulled Clara back to sleep against the hypnotizing sound of the locomotive chugging along, immersed in the intense mid-winter blizzard.

After almost thirty minutes, she awoke with a sudden gasp as the car rocked after going over a rough rail switch. The train began to slow, as it had for the previous stops. Curtis glanced at his pocket watch. The time was now about three in the morning.

Always the gentleman and aware of the commitment he made to her, Curtis stood up and extended his hand to the young lady.

"I believe we've arrived at your destination, Miss. May I help you get off the train?"

He felt the warmth of her smile as she collected her things and re-wrapped her infant in her arms. Clara stood up and accompanied Curtis to the rear of the car, stepping out of the vestibule of the train car into the foot-deep snow.

The bitter cold instantly stung her face as she stared into the dark blindness of the snowstorm, attempting to get her bearings. She pulled her infant closer and wrapped the blanket tighter around its tiny head.

Curtis looked around for a platform or building of some form but could see nothing in the blinding snow.

Her uncle had committed that he would be there to meet her at her stop. But she could see no sign of him. So she and her son began trudging along the tracks through the deep snow toward the front of the train.

Then, with a shudder that shook all the cars, the train pulled ahead, and Curtis stood helplessly in the vestibule, watching the mother and infant disappear into the blinding snowstorm.

Returning to his seat, Curtis closed his eyes and breathed in the remnants of the sweet lavender perfume that Clare had been wearing.

But a few minutes later, the train again slowed and came to a complete stop. Roger, the conductor, came walking thru the train, announcing the arrival at the hamlet Flag stop, and when he got to her seat, he abruptly stopped and stiffened.

"Where did the lady with the baby go?"

"She got off at the last stop," replied Curtis, who had just helped her off the train.

Roger stopped cold; he just stood there, frozen in place with wide-open eyes, as if in a state of total paralysis for the moment.

"She has gone to her death then, for that was not a station. We only stopped the train because we had to fix something that had gone wrong on the engine."

He immediately reached over and pulled the emergency cord, signaling "stop" to the Engineer.

Roger left the train car, went up to the Engineer, explaining the situation, and the train crew backed the train while the conductor went through each car, calling for volunteers to assist in the search.

When the train reached the approximate spot where the woman had departed, all train crew and volunteers disembarked and started to search for her.

In just a short amount of time, the unrelenting snowfall and blowing wind had obliterated any trace that might enable the searchers to tell which direction the young woman had gone. They searched for quite a long time and, at last, someone found her, huddled beneath the branches of an evergreen tree; frozen, covered with ice and snow, with the little lifeless babe wrapped in the blue blanket clutched close to her heart.

Curtis never recovered from that fateful night. Upon reaching his destination in Pittsburgh, he, the other train crew members, and passengers were asked to give their accounts of the incident to the police and B&O officials.

Because of his testimony, the B&O determined Curtis did not have the judgment needed for his new position, and he was dismissed. But the greater loss was the glowing ember of love kindled that night had forever gone out.

Fifty years later, the legacy of that fateful night lived on. Curtis learned a painful lesson about how a person making an honest mistake could result in tragic consequences. He spent his life mourning the beginnings of what appeared to be a promising relationship and had died with Clara and her son, all because of his sense of compassion and kind offer of assistance.

For decades, Curtis had carried the heavy burden of what had happened that day and lived out the remaining days of his life tormented by the first and third parts of Shakespeare's message: "Love all / do wrong to none."

But it never occurred to him that Clara had also forgotten the beginning of that lesson from Shakespeare: "Love all / trust a few."

TERRY THE TRAMP

IT WAS a warm morning on May 3, 1975, when I found myself sitting with several others at a donut shop counter in Jacksonville, Florida.

I had begun the conversation with this stranger with a casual comment, "Looks like we're going to have a nice day." This man, who later introduced himself, turned to me and replied, "No, today is not a nice day, and if you know what's good for you, you'll steer clear of Landing Park today."

I responded, "I'm just in town visiting. May I ask why today isn't a nice day, and what's the deal with steering clear of Landing Park?"

He apologized for his curt response, and

reached out his hand to me in friendship, only introducing himself as Kevin.

Kevin looked like a typical man in his fifties. He turned to me, apologized for the strange greeting, and explained,

"I'm sorry, but May third always leaves me edgy. It's about what I've had to deal with on the job."

"Job?" I asked.

Again, Kevin apologized. "I was a cop, just recently retired from the Jacksonville Police Department."

I nodded and asked, "OK, congratulations on your retirement. But why should I stay away from Landing Park today?"

Kevin looked around the shop and then replied in a low voice,

"Bad things happen to people at that Park on the third of May."

Now my curiosity got the best of me.

"What are you talking about?"

He explained, saying, "What I'm going to tell you has never made it to the police blotter, but I'm as sure about it as one can be. When I joined the force as a rookie patrolman for Jacksonville in 1953, I was assigned a beat along the waterfront of the St. Johns River. I'd been on this beat a couple of years when I watched a groundbreaking along the waterfront for what would become the tallest skyscraper in the Jacksonville skyline. I passed this site two to three times a day when one day I saw something pretty extraordinary.

"Raymond International was the contractor that had been hired to excavate the site and pour the building foundation. I watched with curiosity as the contractors tore down the entire city block along Bay Street, where the Jacksonville waterfront and docks and warehouses once stood at the edge of the St. John's River.

I watched the contractors' machinery driving sheet pilings around the perimeter of the block and then other equipment excavating a huge opening in the ground that looked to me like it was at least three or four stories deep. I was taken by the massive size of this project. I'd never seen an excavation of that size before.

Jacksonville Waterfront

"There was a continuous roar of huge diesel pumps brought in to hold back the water table from the St. Johns River. As if that wasn't enough, there was an ear-shattering sound of steam-powered pile drivers that were hammering huge steel I-beams and hollow pipe casings all the way down into the muck of the riverfront, trying to hit bedrock, from what I was told.

"The noise was unbearable! I couldn't imagine

being around it all day. The roar of the pumps and the loud pounding cadence of the pile drivers made my ears hurt, even if I was several blocks away.

"And then one morning as I was walking along my downtown beat, I heard all the noise stop. I had to know what had happened; had an accident occurred?

"I rushed to the waterfront site and through openings in the high wooden construction fencing surrounding the job site, I could peek in and could see that all the machinery had been shut down and the men below in the hole were scurrying around a trench that was being dug. Apparently, they had struck a large metal object. The crew began to unearth the object using hand shovels and, as they did, you could see the outline of a large railroad steam locomotive begin to appear.

"What was a locomotive doing buried in the muck along the St. Johns River shoreline?" I wondered.

"When the constructions workers realized what they had uncovered, the men stopped digging and huddled around, trying to figure out what to do about this unexpected discovery.

"Was this locomotive of historical significance? All on the job site knew what was at risk. The project manager scrambled up a ladder out of the excavation and ran over to the nearby construction trailer to phone the General Contractor. Apparently, the Contractor then called the owner, who was a large insurance company that had contracted for this new skyscraper to be built.

"Watching from afar, I later learned that the insurance company had reacted quickly. They knew that time was of the essence. If the press got wind of what they had uncovered that morning, this discovery could hold the project up for months, or possibly even stop construction of the building altogether.

"While the phone calls were going on, a group of project engineers in white helmets quickly gathered around the locomotive and based on the outline that was now visible, estimated that this locomotive would weigh in excess of eighty tons. This was relayed to the Contractor, who then notified the owner. The consensus opinion was that recovery of it would be both difficult and expensive.

"In the course of one hour, the insurance company officials that owned the property had decided that there wasn't enough time or money to recover the locomotive intact. Since they wished to avoid unwanted publicity of this finding, the General Contractor was told to leave the engine where they found it and continue to build the project around it. In other words: 'Bury it, before anyone notices it.'

"One hour later, the pumps and pile drivers started back up. But fortunately, as this scene was unfolding, I had continued to move along the fence and gotten close enough to snap a few pictures of this steam engine with the pocket camera I always carried with me.

"Later that day, I dropped off the roll of film at a drugstore, thinking this would be an interesting set of photos to add to my collection. But upon getting the film developed, which took about three days, I noticed, in the photos I'd taken, that there were remnants of a badly deteriorated wooden boxcar that seemed to have been attached to the back of the locomotive's tender.

"Of course, by the time I'd gotten these photos back, the locomotive had already been covered, the building's foundation forms erected, and concrete was being poured. At this stage, the locomotive and the boxcar were now buried deep underground. The few short hours that the train had seen the light of day quickly became a forgotten memory.

"Sad. I would have liked to know a bit more about that train.

"And so I went back to my normal routine. A few months later, I took a promotion and was assigned to a new precinct uptown.

"Frankly, I had all but forgotten about the train incident.

"Several months later, on the third of May, I read a report of a person who was said to have disappeared while going for a walk in the park that had been constructed in front of the new skyscraper. They had disappeared without a trace. The same thing happened the following year, again on the third of May, and again on the next year as well.

"In each of the incident reports it was said that the detectives had identified a 'person of interest,' a foul-smelling tramp, that had reportedly been seen in the vicinity of the park around the time of the disappearances.

"It really shouldn't have concerned me since the riverfront area was no longer my beat. Still, I found the timing of these disappearances curious, and never in my years walking that beat could I recall seeing a tramp in that area that matched that description.

"It got me thinking.

"That beat had been pretty quiet until that building went up.

"I wondered if that construction project may have had something to do with this case.

"Every third of May this was happening. So the following year on that date, I returned to the scene, and met with the detective working the latest disappearance. After we spoke, I walked the area and spotted something that the investigating detective had overlooked.

"It was a shiny new silver dime laying on the sidewalk in front of a park bench. Although it was probably insignificant, I wrote it down in my spiral notepad.

"The disappearances continued on the third of May each year, but the department had established no connection, and the tramp reported in the area had never been positively identified. But, with the pattern of regular annual reoccurrence, I just felt there had to be something more. What was special about the third of May? Each year on that date I started vising the site and each year I found a shiny silver dime laying on the sidewalk in front of a park bench.

"Now, I don't believe in coincidences and I'm a beat cop, not a detective, but I started doing my own investigation. First, I had to understand what was special about the third of May and that location.

"It has taken me years of personal research, but I've pieced together a picture of what might be happening by looking up police reports from several places across the country and scouring other historical records.

"What I believe I've found makes my blood run cold. I did not expect my informal investigation to connect me with that locomotive that is now buried in the foundation for that skyscraper built twenty years ago.

"Here's the story I was able to piece together:

"First, I started looking into what had once existed at the location where people have been disappearing. And then, working with that information, I started going backwards.

"It began on the third of May in the year 1901, when a fellow only known along the rails as 'Slippery Terry' was hiding behind some crates in the corner of a southbound wooden boxcar that was rumbling down the tracks toward Jacksonville's waterfront.

After the cargo for the shipment had been checked and double checked and loaded aboard, the train Conductor walked the length of the train to make sure that the door of each box car was securely closed and latched. But on this day there was some undocumented "additional freight" aboard the train, as the Conductor had allowed a "box car passenger" to scramble aboard as the cars of the train were being assembled.

Despite against the rules, Conductors were known to grant such favors to railroad tramps who had money in their possession.

"'Slippery Terry' was no stranger to law enforcement in several northern cities where he was wanted for a variety of small thefts and scams. Terry was said to have a pocket containing several shiny new silver dimes, which he used whenever he needed help to avoid arrest and jail time. It had worked for him several times in cities up north.

"Mind you, back then, a dime was a lot of money, and a shiny dime could even buy you a pound of bacon. Terry had learned, with a single dime, he could get himself out of any predicament he found himself in. Local cops and jailers were easily influenced when that kind of money got flashed.

"Hobos and tramps of the day had their own set of shorthand symbols and a unique way of writing messages to tell their colleagues, when and in what direction they were traveling. Terry had left a marking on a water tank in Savannah, Georgia that indicated he was heading South on the third of May, which meant his next stop along the rails was Jacksonville, Florida.

"He had hopped a morning freight train, most likely bribing a railroad brakeman in the Savannah rail yards with a dime or two to let him board this boxcar before it was closed up. I'm guessing that with several warrants for his arrest, Terry was figuring once he got to Jacksonville, he could bribe his way onto a freighter headed for Central America where he felt confident that he would be out of the reach of the law.

"I imagine Terry must have felt pleased with himself when he felt the train beginning to slow down and started to back into the sidings of the Jacksonville riverfront docks. These docks were built over swampy marshland to reach the river, and the railroad had laid tracks on the docks, enabling the young City of Jacksonville to conduct trade with the steamboats coming and going on the St. Johns River.

"The locomotive pulling this five-car freight train would have dropped the last four boxcars to their intended dock and warehouse, leaving the locomotive and remaining boxcar with Terry inside, finally arriving at their final stop on Pier 59.

"I can imagine Terry waiting eagerly by the

door like an anxious cat ready to pounce on its prey. All that was left was for the warehouse attendant to break the lock and slide the door open. I'd bet that once Terry saw that opening, he'd be out of the car in a flash, long before the railroad detectives that worked the docks could catch him.

"But the door didn't open. And then Terry smelled the smoke and felt intense heat. How could he know it wasn't the smoke of nearby factories or the hot, humid heat common to Jacksonville? For you see, on the third of May 1901, the Great Fire of Jacksonville had already consumed most of the wooden buildings in downtown Jacksonville and was headed straight for the wooden covered docks along the Bay Street waterfront. Pier 59 was right in its path.

"Earlier in the day, the engineer of the locomotive and his fireman had been keeping a watchful eye out as they threaded their train into the city going between the mostly wooden structures that comprised downtown Jacksonville. They felt a strong prevailing westerly wind that

they worried could toss sparks from their locomotive's smokestack onto the shingled roofs of
nearby wood framed homes and businesses. It
had been a very dry spring in northern Florida
and the last thing they wanted to do is see them
responsible for starting a fire.

But what they couldn't have realized was
that a fire was headed their way. As lunchtime
approached, a few block away, workers at the
Cleveland Fibre Factory had gone to a nearby
home for their midday meal being cooked over
an outdoor fire. Sparks from their fire travelled
over the fence and ignited a rack of dry Spanish
Moss.

"The Cleveland Fibre Factory collected and
treated tons of Spanish moss that were to be
used at that time as stuffing for mattresses and
pillows. It was thought to be comfortable by
contemporary standards and easily accessible to
anyone who could reach it as it hung off many
southern trees. The company took incoming
moss and gave it a quick dunk into boiling water
to neutralize any potential for insect problems,

especially chiggers, and then set the moss out on drying racks. Surrounding the factory were lots filled with racks of treated Spanish Moss being dried for future use.

What Terry could not have known as he felt his train being switched onto various tracks at the waterfront rail yards was that the fire had broken out in the racks of Spanish moss at the factory had become a raging inferno and as it grew it was hurling burning shingles into the adjoining buildings and racing across he downtown area.

"I wonder what thoughts were going through Terry's mind as he peered through the wooden slats of the boxcar and realized that the warehouse workers and train crew who had fled the burning docks had abandoned the locomotive and its last boxcar of cargo.

"None of the dimes he carried in his pocket would help him escape the inevitable. As the flames swept over the wharf, it burned intensely before collapsing into the oozing muck of the riverbank. Likely, the last sound Terry heard was the locomotive hissing and steaming as the muddy river water rushed over it, taking his car down with it. Terry and his pocket full of shiny dimes had reached the end of the line as the dirty, salty, brackish water of the St. John's River filled his lungs."

Kevin paused as the waitress refilled our coffee.

He continued. "Every year since that locomotive was discovered and re-buried, a person disappears without a trace on this day, the third of May. And each year the cops search for clues to the disappearance year after year, but never can find any. Because they always overlook the dime laying on the ground.

"I've kept this to myself for many years, because if I told the detectives my story, they'd lock me up, thinking I'm some kind of nut, don't you think?"

I nodded in agreement; it sounded pretty far out to me.

Kevin could see from the look on my face that I was a skeptic and wanted to go to see for myself.

Kevin pleaded with me, "So, whatever you do on this day, do NOT go there.

"Don't look for a shiny new silver dime lying on the pavement because, if there is one thing I have learned from my research, it will not end well for you!

"You see, my friend, it's my belief that when you pick up that innocent-looking dime, you've just let Terry the Tramp know he has purchased the services of yet another person he can get to do his will. Do you want that?"

THE RACE FOR RATON PASS

THE STAKES couldn't have been higher. In early 1878 the Atchison, Topeka, and Santa Fe Railway (AT&SF) had negotiated the right-of-way to construct a passage through the Raton Pass. It was expensive, but a very strategic play for the railroad that held the key to the main route to the mines and markets of the growing Southwest territory, and also to California and the Pacific Ocean.

At the border of present-day New Mexico and Colorado, Raton Pass was one of the most important, yet treacherous segments, of the Mountain Branch of the Santa Fe Trail. The pass established by the early settlers cut through the rugged snow-capped Sangre de Cristo Mountains and allowed wagons access to the vast and much undiscovered western territory.

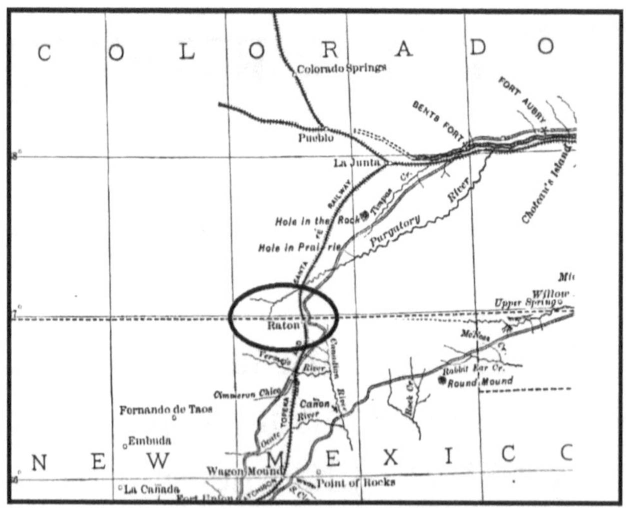

Raton Pass on the Old Santa Fe Trail

The old Santa Fe Trail had evolved from a rugged trail to a road, of sorts, by the mid-1860's.

The "road" was considered "passable" in most places, but only for certain times of the year.

A sound team of horses or mules could handle the steep grades, except near the summit on the Raton side, where, for more than half a mile, the grade became very steep. During the winter or other rainy seasons, the pass was barely usable, as it became little more than a muddy bog, impassible by the teams. The soft shale rock of the area, from which the original road was built, would break down into a bottomless muck, stopping most wagon or stagecoach travel during those periods.

In 1866, "Uncle Dick" Wootten, a colorful local pioneer, owned the rights to Raton Pass. He improved the most treacherous part of the Santa Fe Trail in order to make it more passable year round. He had spent years heavily altering the original trail by grading, blasting, bridge building, and clearing.

When he was done, he had made the trail usable in all seasons for horses, wagons, and stagecoaches alike. That work completed, Wootten, a shrewd entrepreneur, opened the trail as a toll road, which turned out to be quite profitable.

By the 1870's, the Raton Pass toll road that lead from Willow Creek to Raton Creek had become the most important of the passes over this divide. The Santa Fe stagecoaches and other freight wagons heavily used it and depended on it. This caught the attention of the AT&SF Railway, who decided they must have this route.

After intense negotiation with Wootten, the rights were secured, giving the AT&SF Railway an advantage. With other competing railroads looking at different routes through the mountains, they knew they didn't have the luxury of time in order to capitalize on this unique opportunity to build and open a railroad through Raton Pass.

Legal battles over the new rail route into New Mexico came from a competing railroad, the Denver & Rio Grande Railway. They had promised their customers a direct and only route from the East to New Mexico and access to the rich mines in the San Juan Mountains. The AT&SF could become a more attractive option if completed.

The AT&SF's engineers had studied and determined that getting across Raton Pass would be a formidable, but an attainable engineering feat. Picking the right man to lead this project was the crucial factor.

The engineers had identified a route for a two thousand and fifteen foot-long tunnel that would be excavated under the mountain. The geology was an unknown. All involved agreed that it would not be an easy undertaking.

At the point where the plans put the Raton Pass tunnel, the elevation was seven thousand seven hundred and sixty-seven feet above sea level. That would put the highest point on the railroad grade line at seven thousand five hundred and eighty-four feet.

It was a bold undertaking that would take an engineering genius to pull it off. No one had ever undertaken a project of this magnitude.

The AT&SF fortunately had the expertise and experience of R. L. Engle, a talented and gifted Civil Engineer from the company's Topeka office. The railroad company's engineers realized that in order for the company to keep their competitive market advantage, the company needed to get to the other side of the mountain before they could complete such a tunnel.

So they devised a plan to drive a railroad over the mountain, while at the same time a separate crew would construct the new railroad tunnel through the mountain.

This strategy posed an immense challenge. Because of the size and slopes of the mountain, just going "over" the mountain was not an option because no locomotive of the day could scale a slope that steep.

The solution to the problem was a "switchback" design that was developed by AT&SF Chief Engineer A. A. Robinson.

He devised a two and three quarter-mile long line that would zig-zag up and over the mountain and enable the railroad to reach the other side, while the tunnel construction continued.

Engle, now appointed as the AT&SF Division Engineer, was put in charge of the tunnel and fourteen miles of the new AT&SF Mountain Division. His responsibility also included setting the final location and construction of the switchback.

Raton Pass Switchback

If you look at a "switchback" it appears like a zig-zag arrangement rail line. This technique had been used in other places where there was mountainous terrain but none matching the height and steep grades of this undertaking. Using a switchback enabled an ascending train to work its way back and forth up the side of a mountain.

It worked in the following way. The train would run uphill in one direction through a switch and onto a stub ended track. The switch would be thrown and the train would then back up the next leg of the ascent. This was repeated as many times as was necessary to reach the top of the mountain. That's the way the AT&SF got over Raton Pass while the new tunnel was being constructed.

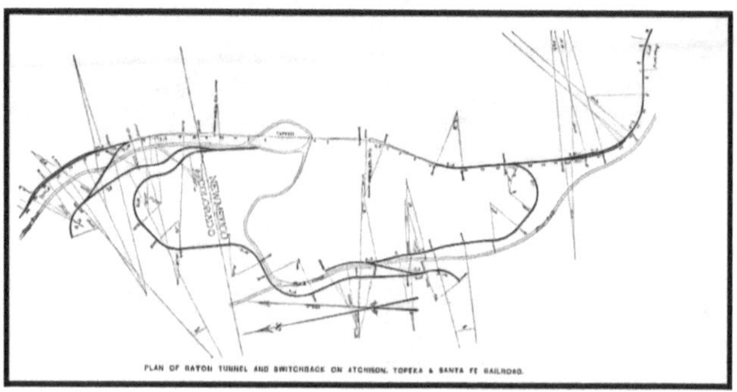

Switchback and Tunnel Plan

Engle's aggressive plan was to have two construction teams working in unison to drive the tunnel through the mountain in order to complete it in the shortest amount of time. At the same time, a crew would be building the new switchback and putting it into service.

But Engle had other major problems to contend with besides the construction activity. The steam engines that were available to run on the switchback were not designed for that type of service, so it needed a different type of locomotive to work Raton Pass.

The AT&SF created specifications for a new

locomotive design that were sent to the Baldwin Locomotive Works.

What they needed was an engine specifically designed for the Raton Pass switchback. This new locomotive, that Baldwin was building, was considered to be the world's largest locomotive, capable of handling the steep grades of this project.

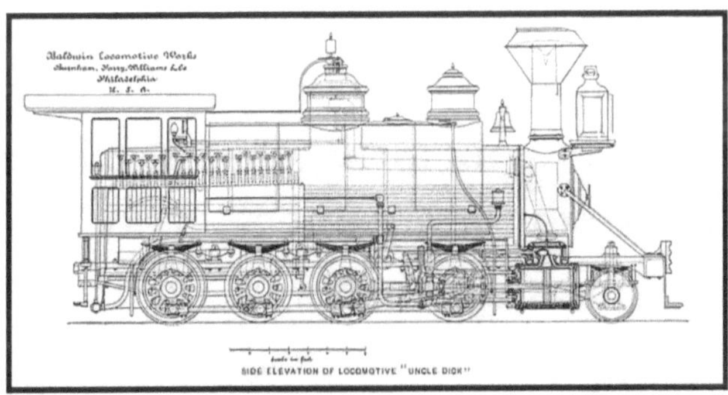

Uncle Dick Locomotive

The AT&SF named this locomotive the "Uncle Dick" for "Uncle Dick" Wootten, from whom the AT&SF had leased this route.

While Baldwin was working on the new locomotive, another problem surfaced.

No locomotive engineer could be found who

had the skill or courage to take the "Uncle Dick" engine over the mountain for the first time.

Fortunately, Engle had many connections in the company, one of whom was George M. Hackney, who was an AT&SF superintendent of motive power. He was the person responsible for the AT&SFs' locomotive operations. Hackney knew all of his talented engineers who had the experience of this risky undertaking. Hackney went right to work on the matter. After some delay and several inquiries, and no engineer that agreed to take this assignment, he located a fireman named Jack Mahoney.

He told him:

"Mahoney, I know you're a good fireman, but this is a new engine, and it's going to be a challenge. If you had a sound engineer at the throttle, would you be afraid to make the trip?"

"Not if you will go along," replied Mahoney.

So a handshake agreement was reached and Hackney and Mahoney became the team designated to take the "Uncle Dick" locomotive and consist over the mountain.

On December 7, 1878, Engineer Hackney and Fireman Mahoney fired up the new "Consolidation" class locomotive and connected it to the first consist of loaded freight cars to go over the Raton summit using the new switchback. This experienced and fearless duo, upon completing this trip, would mark the beginning of a new era in mountain railroading.

Upon reaching the summit, they took the "Uncle Dick" and consist safely down the steep roadway into New Mexico. It was a momentous occasion, celebrated with great fanfare.

The AT&SF had become the first railroad ever to cross over the mountains into New Mexico.

Meanwhile, Engle's construction team had been hard at work on the construction of the tunnels working toward each other.

The railroad tunnel construction work was awarded to the firm of Fitzgerald, Mallory & Flynn. They were selected based upon a solid track record of railroad construction work and their particular skills in tunneling and the use of explosives. On May 20, 1878, Fitzgerald, Mallory & Flynn arrived with an army of men and materials, ready to begin work. Construction of the mountain tunnel literally started off with a bang.

On the first of June an eight by fourteen-foot shaft was started, located one hundred twenty five feet away from the South portal. Thirteen weeks later, tunneling work began at this shaft to drive the tunnel toward the North portal. Tunneling work was now underway in both directions from the main shaft that had been driven.

This army of tunnel workers worked day and night, in two eleven-hour shifts, six days a week, from 6 a.m. Monday to 6 a.m. Sunday. One crew drilled the holes for the explosives using manual rock drills. This type of drilling for blast holes was double - handed work (two man crew) where one man would be holding the drill and the other one striking the drill bit using a 7 to 8 pound sledge.

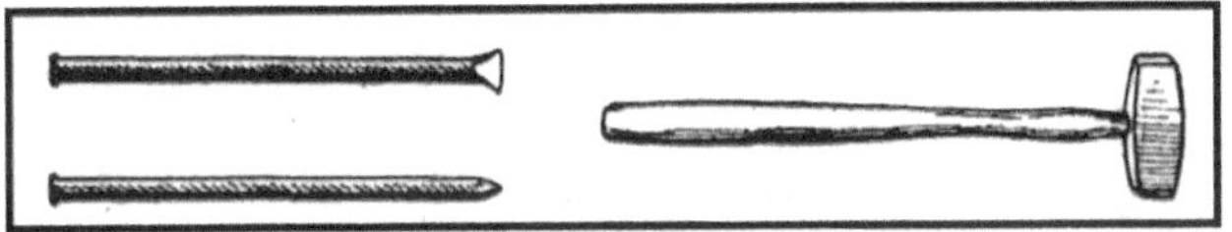

Hand Rock Drill

The crew behind them packed the holes with Hercules Black Powder charges and set them off. Another crew behind them cleared and removed the blast debris. With each blast, the crews clawed their way ahead through the mountain until July 7, 1879, when the tunnel excavations met each other, marking the completion of that phase of construction.

Ballasting crews then came in to lay the roadbed with track-laying crews following right behind them. On September 7, 1879, the track work was complete. The tunnel was deemed ready for traffic, and the use of the over the mountain switchback was discontinued.

The railroad had taken on a huge risk, but it had paid off.

Robert L. Engle had risen to the daunting task at hand, and overcame major challenges that would have overcome a lesser man. In only fifteen months, his teams had done what others said was an impossible undertaking.

The glow of joy on Engle's face warmed all present as he oversaw the last two spikes being driven for the tunnel connection by two employees. With joy in their hearts, all present watched as Engine 27 began the maiden voyage through the new tunnel with Engineer John Bergman at the throttle of the locomotive and Fireman George Sypher working alongside him.

A proud day indeed!

THE TRACKWALKER

MY NAME is Otis, and like most of my young friends living in rural West Virginia, I found adventure climbing up to the railroad track that ran along the steep hillsides behind our houses.

We could connect our little villages more easily by these tracks than by the few primitive roads that connected our communities. Those ribbons of shiny steel gave us access to our favorite places to play, swim, and explore. The railroad tracks provided a direct route to these places, with tunnels going through the steep hillsides and trestles over the rivers, valleys, and streams.

I found the tracks to be a place of solitude. My father was a coal miner, and I didn't get to spend much time with him. When he got home, he was often tired, dirty, and irritable. Some nights he would come back heavy with the smell of liquor, and the house would erupt into angry shouting, leaving my mother crying. When that happened, I found peace walking the tracks.

On one of my walks along the rails, I ran into an older fellow walking the tracks. He differed from the tramps that one would sometimes see carrying a bundle on a stick over their shoulders. While these men also walked the rails to avoid attention, this man was different. He seemed fit and walked upright with a sense of purpose. He carried a satchel on a stick with him, but it had the railroad's name on it.

As we approached each other, he looked up and, glancing at his pocket watch, said, "Son, you might want to get off the track for your own safety. The 10:45 a.m. is coming through in a few minutes."

And with that, he continued down the rails, apparently paying particular attention to the rails and railroad ties and occasionally picking up and discarding a piece of metal debris.

I was glad he said this because the roadbed tapered steeply into a deep ravine on this section of the track. At the next safe spot, I stepped off, and sure enough, right on time, the train came barreling through: It was a huge steam locomotive pulling fifteen passenger cars.

A few weeks later, also in the morning, I encountered the man again on a different section of the track and thanked him for his kind warning last time. My curiosity peaked, and I asked him, "Why are you out here, walking the rails?"

"I work for the railroad, and this is my job: walking the track."

"A job? Do you mean one you get paid for?"

He smiled and nodded his head.

My destination for that day no longer mattered. I wanted to know more about this fellow and what he did for a living.

"Mind if I walk with you?" I asked, to which

he replied, "Not at all, but you'll have to keep up."

I wanted to know more, so I asked,

"What's your name?"

"My name is Oscar. I'm what they call on the railroad a Trackwalker."

"That's kind of a funny job title, but I guess it kinda makes sense," I replied.

As we walked along the tracks, he told me that the railroad hired men like him to do a very important job, to ensure that the tracks and anything the track went across or through were kept safe for the trains that traveled this section.

"The 'Trackwalkers' job is to walk over the track, clearing the track as far as possible ahead of the next train. That involves me watching all portions of the track that could be endangered by any issues with the rails or roadbed, debris of any kind, rock slides, falling rocks, washouts, forest fires, etc."

"Wow, that's a lot of stuff! Is that all you do? Walk all day?"

Oscar laughed.

"Yep, that's all I do every day. Walk, walk some more, and walk even more. An ordinary day's work requires me to walk about twenty miles along this same stretch of track, which is about five miles long. I walk it back and forth twice a day. It's called a 'beat', and you get to know your beat pretty well when you do this day after day."

I noticed the shoes he was wearing had very thick soles. He explained that because he walked over sharp ballast stone for that many miles a day, the soles of his shoes had to be tough. That made a lot of sense to me.

When I asked about his shoes, he told me, "Good shoes are a must, almost as important as good judgment! The railroad depends upon people like me to act properly if anything is found wrong with the track."

I didn't understand.

"What could go wrong with the track?" I asked.

"Sometimes, I find things wrong on the track that would cause a train to derail or wreck. I try to fix as many of these things as I can.

"But there are some problems I cannot fix, and since the railroad runs on a pretty accurate time-table, there are things I must do to try to prevent a derailment or accident. When I find one of those issues, the first thing I do is run ahead up the track and put out a stop torpedo signal on the tracks well ahead of the train that is due.

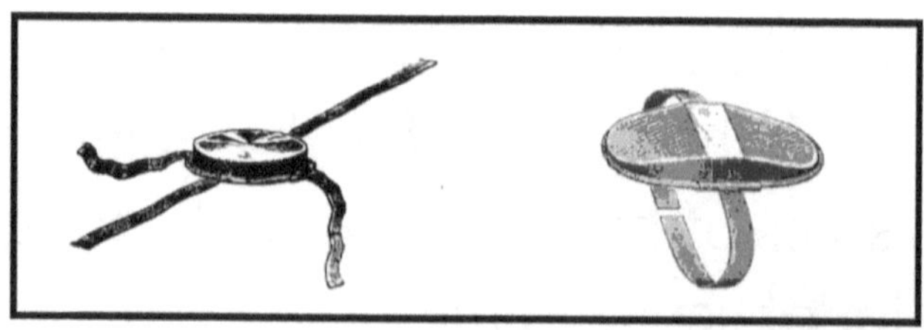

Track Torpedoes

"Then I run back to the danger point and leave a red flag (if it's daytime) or a red lantern (if it's at night) on the track. Then I put a stop torpedo signal out in the other direction at a safe distance, just to ensure that a train doesn't come in the opposite direction.

"I run back to the danger point and go a little

distance toward the inbound train to ensure they have heeded these warnings. I have seen train crews that missed the loud explosions of the torpedo signals, and I have had to stand on the rails waving a red flag or lantern so the approaching train crew could see that they needed to stop!

He could see a puzzled look on my face, so he explained, "A track torpedo is a loud explosive device that is attached to the rails in pairs by a trackwalker or section hand in order to warn an oncoming locomotive that they need to stop the train. It makes a loud bang, but not enough to cause any damage."

I was flabbergasted!

"What kind of things would make you have to do all that?" I asked.

"As I'm walking, I see and can fix lots of smaller stuff every day, it seems. But besides me checking on track conditions, I have to find and report rock slides, washouts, burned trestles of wooden bridges, broken rails, or other dangers. The railroad depends upon me to take action in time to stop the oncoming trains safely. And I take this job very, very seriously."

I really liked the sound of this. I loved the outdoors and the excitement of the railroad; this kind of work sounded wonderful to me. I was near where I was planning to go and I thanked Oscar for telling me everything as I headed down the steep embankment to the dirt road below.

I couldn't wait to learn more, and on days when I was not in school, I continued to run up the side of the hill and catch up with Oscar as he walked the tracks. Each time he told me a bit more about his job and some things he had experienced.

One afternoon, I asked Oscar how he liked his job. He paused, rubbed his short goatee, and told me,

"It's an important but very solitary job. You walk mostly by yourself for several hours a day."

He confided he liked the quiet moments because they gave him time to think; and in his off hours, he enjoyed reading and writing poetry, and added, "I could never stand the confinement of working in the mines, or a factory with all of that constant noise. Here I can be close to nature, and experience life in a way folks down below cannot."

I watched him as he looked up to the birds circling overhead as he continued, "This job has a kind of rhythm to it. But if you like being around people, I suppose you could get lonely."

Oscar told me he would walk the tracks for about six or seven hours each day for his assigned beat.

"The company expects me to be onsite for about ten hours a day, because one could never tell what you'll encounter while walking this beat. Some days, though, I might find nothing special, so I can move along pretty quickly and you'll find me reading a book in my Watchman's shanty."

He explained that at each end of his beat, there was a Watchman's shanty, furnished with a telegraph, a chair, and a stove for cold weather.

The railroad understood they could not expect a man to stand outside and wait during all kinds of weather.

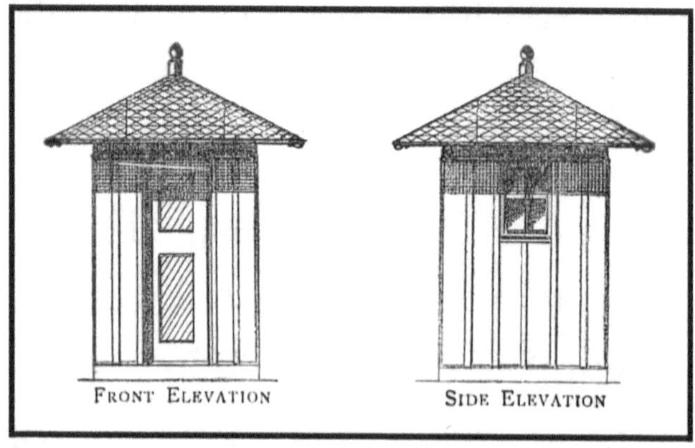

Watchman's Shanty

The next time I met him was at the Watchman's shanty at one end of his beat, where he showed me more about what his job entailed.

Up to that point, all I knew was that the job was about noticing things along the way that a normal person would overlook if they were walking along the track.

He told me about how the company expected him to make adjustments to the track as was necessary. He opened up his leather valise that I'd noticed he always carried with him. Inside was a collection of tools of various types that he carried to meet the needs of what he might encounter.

"All Trackwalkers carry an accurate watch, train schedule, red flag and track torpedoes, and a measuring tape to measure the length of the rail in case I find one that is broken.

"On my beat, there are five trains a day listed on my train schedule, so I have to keep on my toes. Once I complete one leg of my beat and made sure it was clear and safe, I go into my shanty and report via telegraph that the line was clear. Then I wait for the next train to pass."

Inside his valise, he carried a light steel wrench that was useful to tighten loose bolts and a small spike hammer to replace broken spikes or drive down spikes that may have worked their way out of the wooden ties.

We walked over to a nearby switch where he showed me how he would use the pick end of the hammer and clean out dirt or ice that could get packed into the flangeways of the track at switches, highway crossings, and behind guard rails.

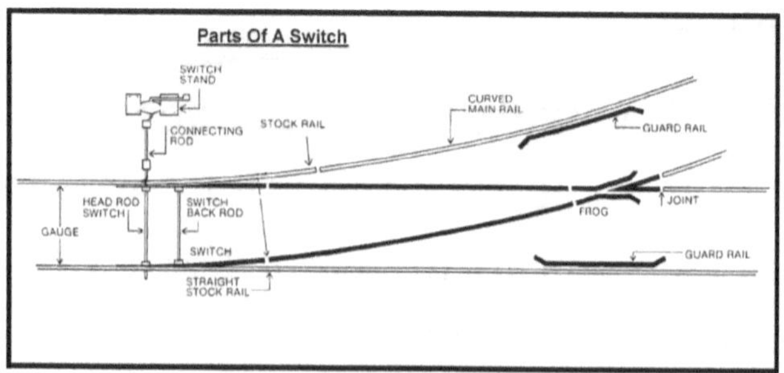

Railroad Switch (Turnout)

Oscar told me that depending upon the weather, he might carry a shovel on his beat to drain puddles of water in the ditches alongside the tracks. In cold weather, he would carry a stiff broom to sweep snow from the points of switches and spring-rail frogs.

Packed snow and ice was a real problem because it could cause a train to derail.

He also showed me another part of his job: Filling and cleaning the switch lamps on each of the switches along his beat.

"My section is pretty easy. I only have eight switches, so it's a fairly manageable task. Now the Trackwalkers, like me, who worked in the rail yards in town have to handle dozens of switches. I'm glad I don't have their job!"

In the wintertime, Oscar said he would light the wicks of each of the kerosene lamps in the switch lights, put them up before dark, and then take them down after daybreak the next morning.

"Lighting a switch lamp when it's windy can get tricky," he told me.

And with a twinkle in his eye, he showed me that the best way to light a lantern or switch lamp in windy weather was to use a piece of soft copper wire he kept in his pocket. It was about eight inches long and he showed me how he wrapped it around a wooden stick match a few turns, making it easier to reach the lamp wick inside.

"Can I try it?" I asked.

"Sure! How else are you ever going to become a railroad man?"

I was learning more about the railroad every time Oscar and I met, and I kept pressing him each time to tell me more.

"The most important task of this job is to keep your eyes on the rails ahead of you and watch for spread spikes on curves," he told me.

"The railroad spikes that hold the rails to the ties are most likely to loosen up and spread in wet weather when the wooden ties are softened; and in the wintertime when the ground is frozen and the ties are held rigidly in their beds. At such times, the places where the track curves are most likely to give you trouble."

He showed me how to pay particular attention to the shims during winter, replacing any that may have worked out of place.

Even though I had walked with Oscar and passed over many railroad devices, I realized I knew nothing about them. I appreciated the time he took to explain the function and operation of each piece of railroad equipment on his beat.

Over the weeks that followed, he also invited

me to watch him as he attended to each frog, guard rail, switch, switch stand, and switch lock. In the hot weather, he explained how important it was to closely watch the moving rails of stub switches and report them to his section foreman when they ran tight.

"I'm not expected to perform the heavier jobs that a Section Crew laborer would do," he explained. "But for light repairs, as I come to them, I can handle those, including replacing broken frog bolts."

"Frog bolts?" I laughed, with an image of a green creature on a lily pad of a pond.

Oscar threw his head back and laughed. He knew I had so much yet to learn, and he was exceedingly patient with me, pointing out the hundreds of details about trackwork I was yet to discover.

"My job is not just about tracks either," he told me one day.

"See those? Pointing up to our right?"

Alongside the tracks, the railroad had miles of telegraph poles, which carried the messages essential to railroad operations.

"As I walk along, I also am looking up at those wires. You see, these wires carry important messages between stations. If I see a single wire that has come down, I'll try to reconnect it. But if it's more than one, I can't fix those, so I have to report the issue to my superiors or the nearest office so they can send out a repair crew out."

Again, another learning moment. I had never thought of the condition of the wires and poles running alongside the tracks. I could now see that these were very important.

His job was to make sure the main line was safe and clear.

Sometimes when he came to a rail siding with cars left, I watched him check several things, and asked him what he was doing.

"It's so important to ensure that these cars put out on the siding are fully clear of the main track," he explained, "I also check to see that the inside track derailing devices are properly set and locked. If someone climbed up on the cars and released the brakes, those cars could go out on the main line. That is what the derailer device is for -- to keep that from happening."

At each occupied siding, I watched Oscar go from car to car to make sure that the doors of the loaded box cars were still locked or sealed.

"The hobos and tramps like to get up in those cars, so they have to be kept locked," he explained.

There were other important tasks this job entailed too!

I was still in school, but what I was learning here seemed far more interesting to me than what I was getting in the classroom.

With each trip I took with Oscar along his beat, I was learning more and more. I learned that his job also involved checking to see that farm gates or any other private opening along the main line right-of-way were closed.

Sometimes he would find livestock that had got through a fence or gate, and he had to find a way to keep these animals off the right of way.

Just when I thought I had seen it all, one day Oscar appeared late at the place where we normally ran into each other.

"I've been putting out a fire," he told me.

"What?"

"In dry periods like now, locomotives throw off sparks, and I'm usually the first to spot them. Part of my job is to try to put out any small fires that may get started on or near the right of way. If a fire has already gone through, I'm the first person to inspect the wooden bridges and trestles to ensure that fire damage hasn't weakened them."

Who would have ever thought that one obscure railroad worker would have so much responsibility?

When I'd get together with my friends and classmates, many of them would talk about railroad Engineers, Firemen and Conductors. To them, these were the "giants" of the railroad.

But I was learning first-hand that there were many "behind the scenes" workers like Oscar that kept the railroad operating day after day.

Over time, Oscar had showed me that the Trackwalker wore many hats, all important duties that fall under the general heading of inspecting the track.

"So you do it all?" I asked one day.

"Oh Lord, no! Each section has a complete Section Crew that handles all the other 'heavier' tasks like repairs and replacements of the mainline and sidings. I just help with the small stuff."

But I knew better. What Oscar did was anything but "small stuff". I learned that working on the railroad was all about teamwork and that everyone had a specific set of jobs to do.

"Each person, whether working alone like me or on a section crew, has specific tasks that are theirs. For example, I'm not supposed to do general track work, such as cutting grass, raising track joints, etc. This is the Section Crew's job."

Oscar shared that while he knew how to do those things, it wasn't his job anymore. In fact, he had come up from a laborer position on the Section Crew. A Trackwalker position was, in fact, considered a nice promotion from the heavy labor work that the section gang did.

"But I am grateful for the years I spent on that gang, because it gave me a good knowledge of track and track work. You really can't do a good job of being a trackwalker unless you understand the track, and that enabled me to properly judge the track's safety, you see?"

"Like what you've been teaching me?" I asked.

"That's only a part of it. There is still so much you have to learn, and that's the thing you learn working on a Section Crew."

"You mean there's more?"

"Well, for example, I started on the Section Crew. Those are the men that work on busy main lines. I had to learn about all types of train signals, hand, flag, lantern, torpedo, and whistle signals. Each of them plays an essential role in the day-to-day operation of the railroad. That kind of important stuff.

"I spent my years doing that kind of work, and when the Trackwalker job got posted, I jumped at the chance. You see, they consider this job a step above that of a section laborer. It has a better work schedule, and it comes with better pay, too!"

Wow! Now I totally got it. It wasn't like I thought when I first met Oscar. It is not just about walking two round trips on his beat twice a day. It was so much more than that.

So, four years later, when I had reached the age where I could apply for a job on the railroad, Oscar told me that the local Section Crew was going to hire a new man. And with a twinkle in his eye, he told me he had told the Section Foreman that he knew just the right fellow for the job.

Right fellow for the job? I couldn't believe what I was hearing!

I was on my way!

SANTA CLAUS ON THE TRAIN

WHAT IS it about Christmas and Trains? There seems to be an unmistakable connection, one that seems to touch our hearts and souls. In my library, I found myself reading a 19th century article about a touching Christmas poem penned by Henry C. Walsh.

Walsh was a journalist with the Altemus Company, a nineteenth-century publishing house in Philadelphia, Pennsylvania. Mr. Walsh, a historian and world traveler, wished to expose the universe to the explorations that he and his colleagues were experiencing through his articles published through Altemus.

Walsh was an original founder of the world-renowned Explorers Club, and loved to write about his daring exploits in Central America and Greenland. But Walsh had other talents that went beyond writing and exploring. There was a side of Mr. Walsh that many did not see. He considered himself a romantic at heart and was always seeking ways to capture and convey powerful and memorable human moments that took the human imagination to places far more interesting than his own personal exploits.

Mother and Child

One of these moments occurred on a cold December evening, with a gentle falling snow. He was sitting on a train station platform, watching people, as he so loved to do. He observed a young mother, dressed in a way that reflected her very modest means, and her little daughter in tow as he watched them board a nearby outbound train.

The sight touched his heart and inspired him to pen an touching but obscure poem he called "SANTA CLAUS ON THE TRAIN".

On a Christmas Eve, an emigrant train
Sped on through the blackness of night,
And cleft the pitchy dark in twain
With the gleam of its fierce headlight.

In a crowded car, a noisome place,
Sat a mother and her child;
The woman's face bore want's wan trace,
But the little one only smiled,

And tugged and pulled at her mother's dress,
And her voice had a merry ring,
As she lisped, "Now, mamma, come and guess
What Santa Claus'll bring."

But, sadly, the mother shook her head,
As she thought of a happier past;
"He never can catch us here," she said.
"The train is going too fast."

"O, mamma, yes, he'll come, I say,
So swift are his little deer,
They run all over the world today; –
I'll hang my stocking up here."

She pinned her stocking to the seat,
And closed her tired eyes;
And soon she saw each longed-for sweet
In dreamland's paradise.

On a seat behind the little maid
A rough man sat apart,
But a soft light o'er his features played,
And stole into his heart.

As the cars drew up at a busy town
The rough man left the train,
But scarce had from the steps jumped down
Ere he was back again.

And a great big bundle of Christmas joys
Bulged out from his pocket wide;
He filled the stocking with sweets and toys
He laid by the dreamer's side.

At dawn the little one woke with a shout,
'Twas sweet to hear her glee;
"I knowed that Santa Claus would find me out;
He caught the train you see."

Though some from smiling may scarce refrain,
The child was surely right,
The good St. Nicholas caught the train,
And came aboard that night.

For the saint is fond of masquerade
And may fool the old and wise,
And so he came to the little maid
In an emigrant's disguise.

And he dresses in many ways because
He wishes no one to know him,
For he never says, "I am Santa Claus,"
But his good deeds always show him.

Of all of the tales of Walsh's worldly exploits, this obscure Christmas poem, crafted by him on that cold bench in the late 19th Century, this may be the one that endures the test of time as it is passed from generation to generation by readers like you.

THE SPIRITS OF TUNNEL 19

IT WAS a rainy Wednesday morning in 2005, as I watched spellbound, listening to the old gentleman at the senior center sharing a personal story to the group he was sitting with.

As he was talking, I realized he was talking about his years working on the railroad. I asked if I could listen in.

"Sure!" he shouted out in a jovial voice, "the more, the merrier!"

In his early 80's, he cut an imposing figure for his age. A full head of silver hair, a neatly cropped mustache, a deep powerful voice, and hands that bore the witness to a life of hard work.

Someone at the table asked, "What was the

one thing you did after retirement that you remember the most?"

A stern gray pall settled over his face and he paused to collect himself.

"That would be the time I went to visit Tunnel 19," he began.

"It was a couple of years after I retired from the B&O railroad. It would have been 1990. In the thirty years I worked as an engineer for the B&O, I'd heard these stories from some of the old train crews about this tunnel deep in the West Virginia mountains. I always hoped I could get that run. It was called the Parkersburg Branch.

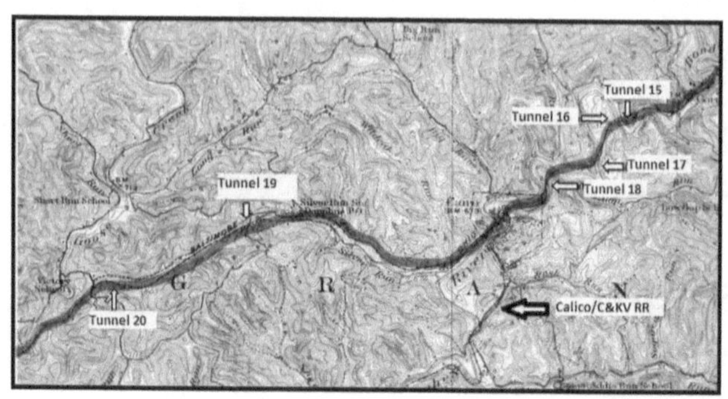

Location of Tunnel 19

"The Parkersburg Branch of the B&O was

considered by railroad men a marvel of modern engineering and had twenty-three tunnels and fifty-two bridges. The route cut through one of the most the rugged parts of the Appalachian Mountain range. This route required bridges and trestles to get across the steep valleys between the mountains. Trains can only handle modest grades, so the route had to be designed so trains could travel on relatively level grades east and west. So impressive was the series of railroad tunnels that the B&O built that even Mark Twain was impressed. It is said that Mr. Twain called the Parkersburg branch of the B&O 'the longest subway in the world.'

"Tunnel 19 was one of a series of tunnels along this branch. It was a huge one measuring one thousand three hundred and seventy-six feet long. The Parkersburg Branch had been a mainstay of the B&O's business since its construction and one I had become very interested in working. I tried bidding on engineer jobs several times. However, I never had the right amount of seniority and was never assigned to that branch.

"By 1985, when I finally had earned enough seniority to bid on that line, the economics of the branch had changed. The company decided to abandon it. Four years later, in 1989, the company had pulled up the track.

"Still, the stories I had heard about this tunnel over the years were burned into my imagination. It wasn't until 1990, two years after my retirement, that I decided I needed to see the tunnel for myself.

"Bear in mind that after years of hearing the stories of the old timers, who were themselves the sons of engineers, this tunnel was the stuff of B&O legends, and I couldn't seem to get it out of my mind. I heard variations in the story over the years, but the constants of the stories were similar - about a series of incidents involving a B&O freight train at that tunnel starting around 1910.

"According to legend, it was late in the day, just

as a bright full moon was replacing the daylight in late October. The B&O locomotive engineer, hauling a sizable freight consist, came around a bend at Silver Run and spotted a young lady with pale white skin and raven hair, wearing what looked like a white wedding dress, staring into Tunnel 19's entrance.

"He blew the train whistle to warn the lady, but knew it was too late. He slammed on the train's emergency brakes, risking a derailment, and with steel car wheels screeching against the rails, the train plowed right through the spot where the young woman was standing.

"By all appearances, his locomotive had hit her."

"I say appear because as the locomotive approached the woman, a dense fog materialized out of nowhere, and the lady seemed to drift up out of the fog, floating over the locomotive.

"Did the train actually hit this strange figure?"

"The engineer and firemen couldn't believe what they had just witnessed. They finally got the train stopped about halfway into the tunnel and worked their way back into the tight space to the tunnel opening.

"The conductor and the brakeman at the rear of the train, unaware of what had just happened, met them outside the tunnel entrance. None of the train crew had seen a body or any evidence that the train had struck a person. There was no clothing, blood, or human remains.

"Finding people on the tracks was not uncommon, particularly in these parts. There were few roads in those days, and those that existed went around the mountains. So, locals often used the railroad tunnels as a shortcut through the mountains. Sometimes people in those tunnels would get run over by trains. But there was always a body. In this case, there was no body, no white dress, nothing.

"At the next tower, they reported the incident and described it as if the fog had swallowed her body."

"But a month after this happened, this same

engineer, on the same run, as he approached Tunnel 19, saw the woman appear again.

"But this time, instead of looking into the tunnel, she was now staring back at him. He blew the warning whistle. Again, the engineer hit the brakes; she never moved. As the train appeared to strike her image, the train crew heard loud shriek, sounding like: 'HELP ME!'

"This time, in addition to the white wedding dress, the engineer and fireman agreed upon what she was wearing; a white wedding dress, golden slippers, and a brooch with ruby red stones.

"Again, no body was found. But, this time, the story of this incident spread among the engineers up and down the line.

"When news of this was telegraphed back to B&O Headquarters in Baltimore, they immediately reassigned the engineer. There was no way the company would put up with ghost stories from delusional engineers.

"They assigned other engineers to this run,

and on nights where conditions were the same, she kept reappearing to them. Again, the trains would slow down, trying not to hit her, and some nearly wrecked trying to stop in time. Railroads ran on tight timetables, and this was disrupting the traffic along the line. Back in Baltimore, the company was running out of seasoned engineers who would bid to work this route.

"Then one young engineer named O'Flannery stepped up. When the company interviewed him, he boldly claimed if he ever saw her, he wouldn't slow down his train, and in fact, would plow right through her. That was the kind of engineer this run needed and assigned him to the run -- delighted to put this ghost nonsense behind them.

"And sure enough, on a night similar to his predecessors' experience, the first time O'Flannery saw her at the opening of the tunnel, he opened up the throttle on his engine and barreled through her apparition and flew into the tunnel.

"A track crew working at the other end of the

tunnel telegraphed the next station that O'Flannery's locomotive had come out of the tunnel with a lady in a white dress laying across the "cowcatcher", the angled apparatus mounted on the front of the locomotive."

Cowcatcher on a Locomotive

"When the Station Agent received this horrific news over the wire, he left his window and ran out to the platform to meet the incoming train. Confused passengers, unaware of the reason for his alarm, also rushed to the edge of the platform, not sure about what they were supposed to be looking for. When the train finally pulled into the station, the Agent and train crew looked all over the front of the engine, but there was no girl, no dress, no blood, just nothing.

"A local reporter who had been waiting at the station captured the scene. While others were milling around outside, he went to the Western Union window and sent a telegram to other papers and wire services about the spectacle that was happening at the station. Overnight, the story of the ghost of Tunnel 19 spread like wildfire.

"Yes, Engineer O'Flannery was also reassigned after this incident.

"Because of the publicity and the legends being spread among railroad men, the company had an even harder time getting engineers to do this run. Reports stated that every engineer who encountered the woman became sick with a mysterious debilitating and deadly illness shortly after their incident with her. This became a major public relations problem for the B&O.

"Some claim the company desperately tried to distance itself from this headache, seeing it as bad for business. Still, as legends go, the stories of Tunnel 19 continued to circulate long after the B&O abandoned this line and pulled up the rails.

"I always wanted to visit the site, but it was two years after my retirement in 1990 before I could get there. I had retired to Florida, and it took me most of a day's drive to the recorded eastern entrance to Tunnel 19.

"Exhausted from the long drive, I should have checked into a motel back in Parkersburg and started fresh in the morning. But when you're tired, you don't always think straight.

"It was getting late in the day and starting to get dark. I had a strenuous uphill climb of about a quarter mile up to the tunnel entrance.

"I was so glad I put fresh batteries in my lantern because I almost stepped on a couple of snakes lying across the path. As I clawed my way through the heavy underbrush, I came upon a clearing, and there it was. I stared at the tunnel's dark and ominous entrance. It was dripping in green moss, and the light from my lantern illuminated thick cobwebs with several large black and brown spiders scrambling about.

"I decided I'd seen enough without entering the dark void. I couldn't imagine there was anything left here but a few snakes. But at that moment, a cold, foul breeze swooshed out of the tunnel in my direction.

"I recognized that sensation. It was the wind coming out of a tunnel being pushed by an oncoming train. The cobwebs at the opening fluttered against the strengthening gust now coming out of the tunnel.

"This is crazy! The tracks are long gone. There's no way a train could be coming through!

"Then just as quick as it started, everything stopped. The rustling of the leaves in the trees that had been very noticeable earlier had stopped, and the chirping of the insects all went silent. The sun had already gone over the hilltops thirty minutes before, and darkness was setting in. The light from my lantern, against the tunnel's opening, showed a dense gray fog starting to appear just inside the tunnel.

"Suddenly, I found myself staring at wispy white orbs appearing in the fog. Those orbs started to transform into ghostly shapes. But these shapes were not only of the lady with the black hair in the wedding dress but also several other figures who had apparently lost their lives in Tunnel 19.

"I'd seen enough, and immediately turned around to head back to my truck. As I did so, I swear I could feel several icy hands touching my back. Now, in a full run, I literally threw myself down the rocky path along the hillside to the space where my truck was parked.

"With a badly shaking hand, I unlocked the driver side door and got into my darkened pickup, locked my doors, settled back into the cold front seat, and let out a loud gasp. I needed a few minutes to compose myself, so I turned on the truck's radio. Hopefully, there would be a nearby radio station with some music that would help me purge from my mind the terrifying experience I just had.

"But Ritchie County was a remote place, deep into the mountains, and the reception was poor. I hit the 'search' button of my radio, but all I got was station after station of static.

"I felt, can this be for real? Nothing on any of these stations?

"And after several attempts, the radio stopped at a clear channel. What I heard was not music or speaking, but a loud whooshing sound, just like the one I'd heard at the entrance to Tunnel 19.

"But the whooshing sound coming out of my truck's speaker faded away and was replaced by a multitude of moaning voices. These moaning sounds became muffled voices, which began to get louder and clearer. Imagine my shock when several voices raised up in unison, in words that I could now clearly hear:

"HELP US!"

THE TURKEY RUN

IT WAS early December 1953, only two weeks after Thanksgiving, when a young warehouse clerk ran into the company's main offices in downtown Omaha, Nebraska. His face was as white as the recent snowfall, and he blurted out, "We have a problem!"

Clarence, the Office Manager, looking very agitated, jumped up from his large wooden desk in his glassed-in corner office, burst out into the large open room, and asked, "And what might that problem be? And why are you bursting in here, disturbing the entire office?"

"Our refrigerated warehouse is full," the young man said, "and we have no space for the incoming poultry arriving today for Christmas and New Year's!"

Clarence shook his head and walked calmly over to the young clerk, wrapped his arm around the clerk's shoulder, and reassured him, saying, "Son, I'm sure there is some kind of mistake. You're new to the company. Let's go out to the warehouse, and I'm sure we'll find the space we need, OK?"

And with that, the two went back into the warehouse. About thirty minutes later, Clarence returned. This time, his face was also as white as the outside snow.

"My God, he's right," he muttered, and went directly over to a small office belonging to the company's Inventory Supervisor.

Through the glass panel of the office door, the rest of the office watched as Clarence was having a very expressive conversation with the Inventory Supervisor. Then abruptly, the door burst open and the two men quickly left the office and went next door to the office of the

Marketing Manager, and the three of them went across to the Accounting Manager's office.

Clearly, something significant was happening. In each of the glassed-in offices that were being visited, heads were shaking, fingers were being pointed, and arms were flailing in the air.

Finally, the four emerged, and Clarence called out to the room in his deep booming voice, "All supervisors and managers into the Main Conference Room, NOW!"

A flurry of activity accompanied the confusion at that moment as all management personnel squeezed through the door into the main conference room. Within a minute, everyone was inside and the door closed and locked from the inside.

Clarence began, saying, "I do not want one word of what I'm going to tell you to go to the two sons until we come up with a solution to this problem."

And with that opening, Clarence described to the room what was happening.

As reported earlier in the day, there was indeed no space for the incoming poultry ordered for the Christmas and New Year's seasons.

Why? Apparently, the company still had about two hundred and sixty tons of unsold frozen turkeys sitting in the company's sprawling warehouse.

At first, the people in inventory management couldn't believe what they were hearing, thinking this had to be some record-keeping error. They sent auditors to the warehouse. It was not a mistake. The frozen turkeys were still there.

It seems the company had significantly overestimated the demand for Thanksgiving 1953, and because of this error, the company had a problem on its hands larger than any it had experienced in its fifty-year history.

This company had been in business for fifty years and had never been unprofitable. The founder of the company had passed four years before and his two sons were now in charge. They knew the business, but had become accustomed to year after year success. They were not known to be tolerant of mistakes. A mistake of this magnitude was unheard of, and one that could cost the company dearly. Unless the company's middle management could find a solution to this problem, a significant financial loss was certain, a first for this company. Such a loss would mean that many would lose their jobs.

By this time, all in attendance clearly understood the dire situation. But at this moment, nobody had any ideas how to fix this mess. The "million-dollar question" on everyone's mind and face was, "What do we do with the two hundred and sixty tons of unsold frozen turkeys?"

As the staff slowly returned to their desks and offices, Geoff, a company railway clerk who was picking up some shipment paperwork, overheard the conversation and spoke up and said, "I believe we have ten company-owned refrigerated railroad cars. Why don't we load the turkeys into them? That would get you the space you need, right?"

The Traffic Manager said, "Yes, we do, and according to my records, they are empty, not currently committed to any orders, and sitting on the tracks right here in Omaha."

Boxcars on a Siding

You could hear a large sigh of relief across the room.

All in the meeting agreed.

"That's a good idea; let's move the turkeys into those refrigerated cars. That will free up the space we need!" someone said.

But then Geoff spoke up, saying, "That's fine, and I'll get them moved to the warehouse siding, but you understand that in order for the refrigeration units on those cars to work, the car has to be moving?"

Clarence and the others looked at each other confused. Apparently, no one in the office other than Geoff knew that important fact.

Clarence said, "OK, let's get them hooked up to a locomotive and get them moving."

Geoff replied, "Where do you want me to send them?"

The room got very quiet again. No one had come up with a solution to this problem, let alone how much time it would take to put it into action. Clarence turned to Geoff and said,

"It's really important we keep these birds cold, so we can't send them south. Let's send them east!"

"East, OK. How far east?"

"As far as we can go, OK?" barked an increasingly-irritated Clarence.

And so that's what Geoff did; he created a manifest and waybill to send the ten carloads of frozen turkeys to Boston and sent it over to the railroad. While waiting for the cars to arrive at the warehouse, the warehouse manager had conveyors setup to load the cases of turkeys onto the railcars. The loading dock was a swarm of activity.

While that was underway, Clarence and the other managers examined their options. Calls went out to their usual large customers, trying to get them to take more turkeys, but these efforts proved fruitless.

With each hour that passed, the management team looked more and more frustrated. Despite coming into the Christmas holiday, the office lights burned well into the night. Everyone knew what was likely to happen if they couldn't find something to do with the turkeys, and knew that instead of Christmas bonuses, many would likely get pink slips.

The turkeys, by now, had begun their cross-country odyssey, as the question remained in everyone's minds: "What do we do with them now?"

Four days later, Geoff got a call from the railroad that the turkey train was pulling into the Boston rail terminal. He had intentionally written the waybill with no destination pickup information, and the railroad needed further instructions.

Geoff went back into the main office, and as before, they had not yet found a solution. He asked Clarence what to do and got the curt reply, "Bring 'em back!"

They sent new shipment orders to the railroad. The "Turkey Train" was turned around in Boston and now began its return journey to the company's siding in Omaha.

Geoff, watching this saga unfold, was slightly amused. He made a mental note that this was not his new infant son, now a year old. He had been a cranky baby and the only thing that would give the parents some peace was putting their son in his stroller and pushing him around, hoping the child would fall asleep. It usually worked. But in this case, the company's middle management in Omaha was getting crankier and more worried by the hour, and a stroll wouldn't improve their demeanor.

Now three days away from Omaha, everyone knew that these turkeys in transit were going to begin to thaw. Time was of the essence, and a very uncomfortable conversation with the two sons loomed on the horizon.

Amid this tension, a young $200/month salesman for the company stepped forward with an idea. He had spent five years as an Army officer during World War II and was familiar with the three compartments of an Army Mess Kit, which basically served a "mess" of food. After the war, he had been a passenger on a Pan-Am flight, where he was served a three-compartment prepared meal on the flight.

He came to Clarence and pitched a new idea: "Let's take these birds returning in a couple days, cook them, and create a pre-packaged frozen turkey meal with corn-bread dressing and gravy, peas, and potatoes, both topped with a pat of butter? Something that the housewife would just have to pop into the oven and reheat."

He stepped over to the conference room blackboard drew a sketch of the tray the airline had served him on the plane..

The purchasing manager spoke up,

"I had a salesman last month that showed me a new disposable aluminum tray they're making that looks like that drawing!"

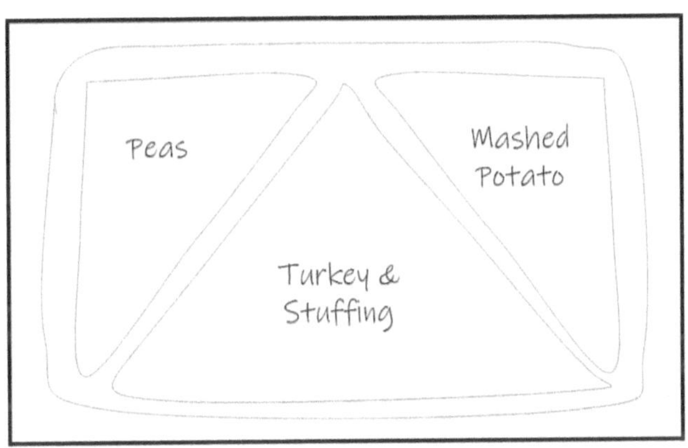

Proposed 3 Section tray

But Clarence was not yet convinced.

"Would anybody even buy such a thing?"

The Marketing Manager piped up, saying, "Remember the chicken pot pie we created last year? We did a market survey before we decided to start that product. What we found was interesting. The men weren't all that thrilled, because they have been used to coming home after work to a home-cooked meal. The women, however, who had to prepare supper loved the idea, and guess who shops for groceries?"

By the salesman's rough estimate on paper, he figured there was more than enough turkey to make five thousand of these frozen dinners, and threw the idea out to the room.

"Five thousand frozen meals? Are you crazy? How do you think we can sell that many of those?"

But Geoff, the railway clerk, who had been listening to the discussion, spoke up, saying, "A year ago, I just bought a television set. Since then, I've been glued to the thing. I'm able to actually watch my old radio favorites like Arthur Godfrey, Jackie Gleason, George Burns and Gracie Allen, and Milton Berle. And there's these great shows like, 'Dragnet' and the 'Ford

Theater.' My wife loves to watch 'I Love Lucy,' and the kids are always watching the cartoons and Superman. It's hard to tear any of us away when it's time to come to the dinner table.

"I'll bet people would love the idea of being able to watch their favorite shows in front of the television while eating dinner!"

Hearing this, Clarence and the Marketing Manager huddled at the end of the huge conference table.

Clarence was feeling a glimmer of hope, and that hard pit in his stomach was easing up a bit.

"Will someone please tell me how we'd even sell such a thing?"

This time, the Marketing Manager, who had been deep in thought, stepped up, saying, "Many of us have bought televisions, and I've noticed that these programs have sponsored advertisements. From what I've seen myself, these advertisers mostly are automobile companies, soap companies, oil companies and cigarette companies. I'm not seeing any food companies.

Family Watching TV

"We could advertise these meals on television, and I don't think we'd have much competition at all. And if you price it for less than a buck, I think people will buy it."

Everyone around the large oak conference table nodded their heads in agreement.

A broad smile spread across Clarence's big round face for the first time. In his mind, he saw how this could play out nicely, thinking, "This could work. It would save all of us a lot of embarrassment, and maybe our jobs. And if it works, we can take the credit for it. And if it doesn't, losing a railway clerk and salesman isn't such a big deal. We'll just say it was their stupid idea."

And turning his attention back to the table, Clarence stood up, gave each manager present specific assignments, and by the time the turkeys arrived at the siding, a complete production line had been setup.

The company had rolled the dice, and found a way to utilize the box cars of unsold turkeys into a new product, and everybody kept their jobs. The two sons recognized the ingenuity and teamwork of the people involved, and saw how they had turned a major miscalculation into a successful new product launch.

One never knows what will happen when you introduce a new product to the market.

Just as the market forecasts for Thanksgiving 1953 had proved wrong, so were the estimates of being able to sell five thousand of these new-fangled frozen dinners. By the end of 1954, the first full year of production, the Company, Swanson Foods, sold ten million frozen turkey dinners, and took its place in history, credited with the creation of the TV dinner.

Amid this story, there was an "unsung hero" who never got the recognition he deserved, and who played a critical part in this success story.

The villain of this story was time. And were it not for the quick thinking of Geoff, the railway clerk that bought the management team the time they needed in order to come up with a solution, this historic development might never have happened.

CAN'T BE HOME FOR CHRISTMAS

EVERYBODY WAS anxious on this blustery Christmas Eve, in 1924, at the young family's home on the side of a hill overlooking the Williamsport, Pennsylvania rail yards. The family sat about, telling stories and eagerly awaiting the tantalizing aroma of suppertime at the family's traditional Christmas celebration, but something important was missing.

Grandpa and Grandma Smith had come to celebrate Christmas Eve with their son, Luke, and daughter-in-law, Bess, at their home, eager to spend the holiday with their grandchildren.

But as the evening meal approached, something was amiss, and all present could feel a sadness in the gathering.

Luke, the children's father, was not there.

He had been called into work that afternoon by his boss due to a fire that had broken out at the Williamsport Machine Company, where he was a supervisor.

Grandma and Bess were busy in the kitchen preparing the sumptuous feast, leaving the others sitting around the spacious living room, listening to the hiss, crackle, and pop of the roaring blaze in the fireplace. Those brave enough to do so crept closer to the hand-laid stone hearth to watch the sparks fly up the chimney. On the opposite side of the room was the straight and heavily- decorated Christmas tree, carefully adorned with the family's handmade ornaments that glittered in the fireplace's hue.

Sarah, the youngest, piped up, saying, "I'm unhappy that Dad couldn't be here with us tonight!"

The other children nodded quietly, sharing her thought.

Sensing the somber mood of the children,

Grandpa John said, "Kids, that's why your dad works in a factory instead of on the railroad. When I was your dad's age, I had seen too many Christmas Eves where I got called out to work. There were many nights when I couldn't be with my family for Christmas."

Grandpa John paused.

He sat there in silence for a moment, thinking about the lesson he had taught his son, reflecting on how unpredictable railroad life had been for him and how often he had thought about taking on a different line of work. But he had stuck with it, endured the difficulties, and tried to pass along his experience to his only son. John let loose a loud sigh and shook his head, realizing that all of his efforts still hadn't paid off. The reality of the situation tonight was no different. His son was at work instead of celebrating Christmas with his family.

Phyllis, the youngest, broke the uncomfortable silence.

"Really Grandpa? Can you tell us what happened?" She asked.

The other children nodded and pleaded like-wise.

He smiled in agreement, paused, reached over to the side table and collected his favorite bri-ar pipe. With his rough and calloused hands, he slowly opened the tobacco tin and with all eyes on him, he carefully filled and packed the deep bowl of the pipe with his favorite tobacco, Altschul's Mixture. Striking a stick match on the side of the chair arm, he slowly lit the pipe, drew it in until it was well lit and waited until its fragrance and faint cloud swirled around his bearded chin.

"I remember clearly the first time I missed Christmas with the family. It was forty years ago, Christmas 1884. It was a very special day. Your father had just started walking on his own and was so excited about Christmas.

"Working on the railroad back then was quite different from what it is today. I was very ex-cited about being able to spend Christmas day at home and enjoy watching my son's very first

Christmas. And to make sure I could do that, for the previous two weeks, I had put in upwards of fourteen hours a day on the road. The company promised me that because I had put in this extra duty, I could certainly spend Christmas day at home.

"But that was not the way the railroad worked.

"It had been a blustery Christmas Eve day, and late in the evening, there was a sharp rap on the door of our cozy little hillside cottage overlooking the bustling community of Williamsport.

"Williamsport had become one of the most prosperous cities in Pennsylvania, and the United States, because of the booming lumber trade. But by 1884, the city had also become quite important as a gateway for the Pennsylvania coal industry. And the Pennsylvania Railroad, my employer, was quite busy.

"It was about 11:00 p.m. when there was a loud knock at the front door. Grandma and I had just put your father to bed and we had finished placing his presents under the Christmas tree.

Who might that be? We glanced at each other, already knowing the answer.

"When I answered the front door, the short stubby Irishman, Tommy Ryan, was standing there. I knew Tommy. He was an old soldier who the railroad had hired as a 'railroad caller'. It was his job to contact railroad personnel when they were needed. During the Civil War, Tommy had gotten injured and still walked with a painful limp. Whether or not it was the war injury, I do not know; but as usual, he was the same irritable person I had encountered before. I wondered if he was ever at peace with himself or, for that matter, the balance of mankind.

"Tommy stood there in the doorway, rocking back and forth, fidgeting in the freezing cold. He said the heavy storm brewing down in the valley and up in the mountains was creating extra work for the engines. He handed me a slip of paper that made it clear, in no uncertain terms, that I would have to leave immediately, pick up a locomotive, and take a special 'blue coal' freight from the Williamsport PA yards up through Elmira, New York's Southside yards to Sodus Point, New York, on the shore of Lake Ontario. Anthracite, or 'blue coal', was the most popular fuel for heating homes and other buildings in the northern states back then, and it had already been a long, cold winter. This special train was supposed to be assigned priority track rights as this shipment was destined for the coal docks at Sodus Point, on the PRR's Sodus Bay Branch.

"Closing the door on Tommy, I shook my head. I had been watching the deteriorating weather that day and it was the one thing that worried me the most. Despite the assurances, I realized I might get called out.

"Your grandma saw the scowl on my face and knew from experience what it meant. Without a word, she went into the kitchen and began preparing my lunch pail.

"You see, Williamsport was an essential connection between the coal fields of central Pennsylvania with Sodus Point, New York, where a large railroad coal dock extended out into Lake Ontario. And the Pennsylvania Railroad had established a direct route from the Pennsylvania coal fields to the waiting ore freighters that would ship the coal to important ports along the Great Lakes.

"It was a run that I'd made many times before. It involved a trip of about a hundred and sixty miles, up through the mountains of central Pennsylvania, across the state line to Elmira, New York, then north to Watkins Glen, New York, up along Seneca Lake, and finally turning Northwest to Sodus Point.

"I collected my kit and, with my tools and lunch pail in hand, I kissed your grandmother, left our house, and headed down to the Williamsport rail yards around 11:30 p.m. against the sting of the snowstorm. As I headed down to the yards, I can't tell you how sad I felt.

"Some way to spend Christmas, I muttered under my breath, realizing this Christmas was a once-in-a-lifetime moment that I could never recover. But the job was the job. It had always provided a steady paycheck for my family, after all.

"In those days, locomotives were seldom not ready for their crews at the terminal, so first, I had to report to the engine house foreman and then go over to the roundhouse to get an engine.

"The regular engine usually assigned to me had been put on another train earlier in the evening due to the snowstorm, so I ended up with one that appeared not nearly in as good a condition as the one I usually ran. My locomotive was sitting outside the Pennsylvania Railroad roundhouse on Walnut Street. After my Fireman and I checked it out, I went with my conductor to the yard office to get my train orders.

"By the time I got the train orders and we got our load of coal cars and the caboose hooked up to the locomotive, it was almost 2 a.m. when we finally pulled the train out of the Williamsport yard.

"The light snow squalls that persisted throughout the day quickly became a blinding snowstorm swirling down the mountains.

"Right off the bat, I realized that the locomotive I'd been given wasn't working properly, which meant a lot of extra work for the fireman and me to get it up to speed and keep it running properly.

"We hadn't gone more than thirty miles north, and shortly after receiving new train orders at Ralston, we felt a sudden jerk. The bell on the engine began to ring, and I knew the train had broken in two.

"By broken in two, that meant that two of the cars had come uncoupled. A bell cord went from the engine cab and ran over the tops or sides of all the cars, all the way to the caboose at the end of the train.

"These weren't the kind of steel coal hopper cars you see on trains today. The cars we hauled back in the day were an adaptation of the "coal Jimmy" cars at the nearby mines that had short wooden sides attached to steel railcar frames.

"The coal cars on my train were slightly larger than the four-wheel "Jimmy" cars, and each carried a load capacity of about ten tons of coal.

"They didn't use the kind of couplers to connect the railcars as trains use today but each car on this train was connected to the next by an eye on one end of the car, and a hook at the other end.

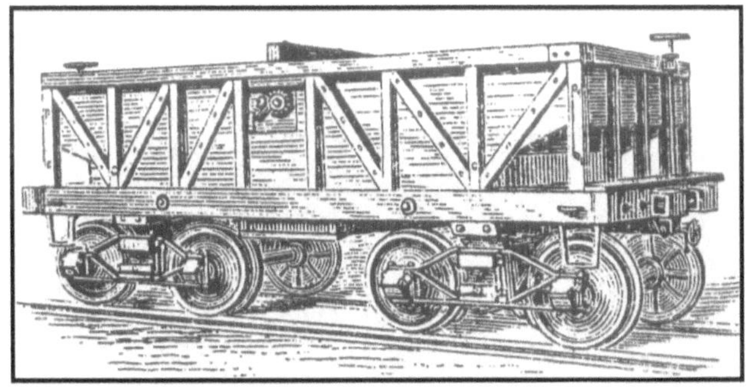

Coal Car

"This type of connection between these coal cars was called a 'draw hook and chain' coupling method, a primitive type of connection that was used by several railroads serving the Pennsylvania coalfields at that time.

"So when you heard the bell clanging in the engine or caboose, the train crew knew there was a break in the train. This was a common problem with these coal cars, where a number of things could cause the coupling to become undone. Going over a rough section of track or a tight curve, or going over a switch can cause these couplings to become undone."

Grandpa set down his pipe for a moment.

Every child's gaze was now riveted on Grandpa.

"What happened next?" one asked.

After repacking his pipe, he continued, saying, "Here's where it got interesting!

"So first, while the train was still moving, the first task was to figure out where the break in the train happened. Then we had to put the two parts disconnected from the train back together.

"As you might imagine, it took the skill of the entire train crew to pull it off. You might think, why not just wait for the disconnected part to catch up? Well, it's far trickier than that.

"First, we had to figure out how far back the

train had broken. Since we didn't know how fast the detached part of the train was going, we knew we had to keep the train moving, while one of us had to go back to the place where the train broke apart, and see where the other part of the train was.

"Meanwhile, my brakeman, whose job it was to set the brakes, was in the back part of the train. When he heard the bell clang back in the caboose, he knew right away what he had to do.

"He left the caboose and crawled forward over each of the loaded coal cars, manually setting enough of the brakes using the iron hand wheel on each car to slow down and hold the rear end of the train. At the same time as I heard the bell in the locomotive, I had my fireman take over the throttle of the locomotive. I crawled back over the coal tender, jumping onto the first coal car that, like most of those cars, tended to rock side to side. I then crawled over the loose coal in each car and, getting to the end, had to jump over to the next coal car, and so forth until I finally found the break in the train.

"The hook on the car I was in had disconnected from the other cars and the connecting chain had snapped. I watched the back part of the train in the distance disappearing into the blowing snow. There was no way to communicate between the front and back ends of the train except by railroad lanterns, and in the snow squall, they were of no use.

"Meanwhile, my fireman, who was still in the engine, was keeping the front part of the train moving ahead so the 'disconnected' back end of the train wouldn't crash into the front end of the train and cause a deadly derailment.

"So as the brakeman in the back section of the train started to apply the brakes to each car, starting with the end of the train, so that part of the train could begin to slow down. I started working with the brakeman, who was now on the lead car of the detached section, signaling me with his lantern, and I was signaling with a lantern to the fireman up in the locomotive. Working back and forth like that we finally matched the speed of the two halves of the train and then carefully brought the two sections together and brought the train to a halt.

"Then the brakeman climbed off the train and re-made the connection.

"This was not only time-consuming but also a dangerous process, as you can imagine. Sadly, that event was just the first break apart of several that occurred that night, and each time we had to go through a similar process before we got the train up to Sodus Point.

"And how long do you think it took us to make that 160-mile run? Well, in good weather this run would normally take me about ten to twelve hours. That night it took me and my crew almost a day and a half, all because of the problems we had encountered."

The kids looked up.

"All of this because of bad couplers?" one asked.

"No, that was only part of the problem that night. It wasn't just the broken couplings or the delays caused by the snowstorm. All the railroad equipment we ran back then was so much inferior to the railroad equipment that exists today. The engines we had were small and lightweight, the water and coal capacity of the tenders was small, and there was no way of taking on water while the train was in motion. So, frequent stops for coal and water were necessary.

"As I told you, the coal cars in our trains had those primitive and unreliable couplers, and there were no automatic airbrakes like trains have today. Each car had a manual brake that needed to be set by the brakeman. These early locomotives were also very difficult to handle. Going through the mountainous Pennsylvania terrain in a heavy snowstorm with this light engine, I also had to use a lot more sand to maintain traction to the wheels of the locomotive. It was a very demanding, physical job for everybody getting this coal shipment through to the coal dock. But we got there, albeit several hours late, finally pulling my train into Sodus Point.

"After emptying my load of coal cars at the

Sodus coal dock, I turned in my engine at the Sodus yards, grumbling at how awful this Christmas had turned out.

"At that moment, I realized that the good pay of being an engineer could never compensate for what I lost that Christmas.

"And I vowed that my new son should not have to make this kind of sacrifice for an employer that was only concerned with schedules and profits.

"So here I was, task completed, sitting in upstate New York, pondering what the quickest way to get back home might be so I could enjoy what was left of my belated Christmas with your grandma and the rest of the family.

"It was a full day and a half later before I finally got back home to my family in Williamsport. I must admit that on that return trip back home, I wasn't a pleasant fellow to be around.

"But my heart jumped for joy as I walked into my house. With your grandmother and my son sitting at the dining room table, I finally got to sit down with my family to claim my share of what was left of the Christmas turkey.

"After my experience and the loss of time with my young family on that precious 'First Christmas,' I vowed that no son of mine should ever have to experience the loss of this irrecoverable 'precious moment.' I'd do everything in my power to keep him from working on the railroad.

"You see, despite the glamour of working for the Pennsylvania Railroad or any other railroad, when a man takes such a job, he commits his life to being on call whenever the railroad needs him. You can never expect to celebrate any life event with your family to happen on the day it should be celebrated.

"For me, looking back on that night, I did what was needed. I responded to what the railroad considered an emergency. I learned the hard way that there were many things beyond my control. I couldn't control the equipment I had to work with, the track conditions, the way

I had to run trains, the way the company made assignments and other things as well.

"I learned that when a trainman left home, I could never count on getting back home at a certain time.

"I wanted your father to have a better life than that."

Just then, the front door opened, and an exuberant dad burst into the room shouting, "Everything is back under control! Let's get this Christmas celebration underway!"

As he headed to the dining room, he beamed with joy as he cast his twinkling eye to his father sitting nearby. The two exchanged a simple grin and a knowing smile. Apparently, the lesson had been learned.

THE YEGGMEN

WHEN I was a kid, I experienced the fears of the unknown that were common to most kids my age; fear of the dark, getting robbed, the death of a parent, and, of course, monsters. And like most kids, I never confided in my mom and dad that these kinds of things worried me.

My dad had spent several years as a brakeman working on the Delaware, Lackawanna & Western Railroad (DL&W), and I used to love it when he'd take me down to the yards. He provided my early education into the ins and outs of the railroad. He was a "giant" among men in my mind, for I came to understand that he did one of the most dangerous railroad jobs of any railroad employee. And he had a reason for showing me these things.

Dad had described to me in great detail about the kinds of tasks that he had to do as a brakeman. Hearing about those things in real life gave me the chills. This wasn't the illustrated characters I'd watched on animated cartoons on television. This was what my dad did. That alone was scary enough to give me nightmares. But when he told me of other relatives who had gotten killed or maimed doing similar work, those images became etched in my imagination. Being around trains was dangerous! A person who was not "on the ball" could get killed! And that was the very idea my dad wanted to impress upon me as he told me these things.

"Son, there are many dangers associated with railroad life," he once told me, "I've told you stories of what I had to do, and about accidents and deaths that have happened in our own family. But I haven't said much about the number of close calls I've had myself."

Something I always looked forward to was when Dad would take me down to the yards to watch these trains coming and going, switching operations, dropping cars off, and making up new trains. I wondered what he wanted me to see. He had already shown me daytime railroad operations, and explained how being a brakeman in the early 20th century was very different then than it was by the 1950's.

He had explained in detail how brakemen did their job back in the twenties and thirties, coupling and uncoupling cars in the crowded rail yards with only inches between them and the passing trains. To stay alive in those yards, you had to be on the lookout for danger every minute. A brakeman had to do these tasks in the railyards but also had many jobs to do on a moving train on the main line. These jobs were different, but much more dangerous.

Sometimes a train's couplers would fail, or a sag or curve in the track, would result in breaking the train into two parts. In the days before automatic air brakes were on all trains, the brakeman would have to climb over the tops of each of the moving railcars to operate the hand-brakes of each car in order to bring the detached part of the train to a stop.

I was amazed and shocked to realize that he did these things day and night, in all types of weather, for many years, and yet, still came home to us safely.

But I had a hunch that this visit to the yards was going to be different. I was about to learn another aspect of his job that showed me just how deadly the job of a brakeman could be.

It was a chilly evening in October 1958, when we had just finished supper, Dad told me to put on my jacket and go out to the car. We were going to take a ride. We drove across town to the rail yards we had visited before, but he said this visit was different. He wanted to show me what happened there at night. He said I would see things that only become visible at night.

"Tonight, son, I want to show you a part of my

job as a brakeman that you can only understand if you see it."

Perched on an embankment overlooking the Erie rail yards, he didn't say anything but just told me to keep my eyes open. He was right. The scene was indeed different.

In the daytime, as trains were moving through the yards, he'd pointed out the trackwalkers, switchmen, and brakemen, each with their assigned duties, walking the rails, throwing switches, and coupling and uncoupling cars. In previous visits, he had pointed out each of these people to me, described what they did, and took me down and introduced me to several of them.

But as nighttime fell, the yard took on an eerie glow, illuminated by the huge metal towers with bright yellow sodium lights shining down. It felt like I was watching another world.

The first thing I noticed was that nighttime railroad operations were less busy. Except for the occasional locomotive switching cars heading back to the engine house, there was far less traffic in the yard than I'd seen during my daylight visits.

However, there appeared another kind of traffic, which was far more apparent to me.

Dad watched me intently and asked, "What do you see?"

Scurrying about in the shadows were men: dozens of them, like mice, running from the bushes that lined both sides of the rail yards toward the boxcars that sat on various tracks. These figures seemed very practiced and cunning, skillfully avoiding being seen by the brakemen and railroad detectives working in the yard at that hour of the night. As trains passed through, they seemed to disappear into the night.

I asked Dad, "Are those railroad tramps?"

Dad laughed and replied, "Son, you've been watching too much Red Skelton!" And he was right. My only experience with any "knights of the road" was the loveable "Freddie the Freeloader," the tramp character that I watched on Friday nights on TV.

"Freddie was a hobo, not a tramp," he pointed out. I looked surprised.

"Oh, there is a very big difference!" He told me that Americans had always had many "homeless" itinerants considered by society as "undesirables." These unfortunates were referred to as Hobos, Tramps, or Bums.

He continued, saying, "People often envision a hobo as a man seen hopping on freight trains to get from one place to another, riding the rails while carrying all his personal belongings tied in a bandanna suspended from a stick over his shoulder. While that's not untrue, hobos are often simply men who found themselves out of work and whose families have been displaced.

"They are most often found in hobo camps near the rail yards in bands of about half a dozen men. The men you're seeing scampering about are from the hobo camps nearby and are trying to hop onto their next ride, looking for boxcars whose doors aren't yet closed and secured.

"In reality, in most cases, many are just down on their luck migratory laborers who work their way across the country, taking whatever kind of work available that the man has the skill or ability to do.

Hobo Camp

"If you listen to hobos talking in their encampments, you'll generally find them using first-rate English, as many hoboes are well-educated, and most can at least read and write.

"I've found that most of the hobos I've met are pretty genial, resourceful, and good cooks. They are skilled 'scroungers' that know where and how to get what they need to survive. They'll go through the community's alleys and gardens in the daytime to collect items for the evening meal. At their encampment, they get together and do their cooking over a three-stick fire.

"Tramps, however, are a different breed. If a tramp can avoid work, they will. Most tramps are drifters who are traveling from place to place, often on foot and occasionally by rail. Hobos tolerate them but don't care much about them because of their lazy ways, and they tend to steal from the hobo or anyone else that's handy. A tramp is not above using thievery or a con job to get along, and they can't be trusted. Even if offered employment, most tramps would turn it down.

"Now Bums are just different. They are homeless, shiftless men who are too lazy to travel and have no interest in finding work. Most of them tend to be alcoholics.

"I'd run into these characters when I was cutting cars or putting trains together. I often would see hobos sitting boldly in open boxcar doors of departing freight trains, waiting to be carried off to their next destinations.

"We brakemen would call these fellows 'happy hobos' because, despite their problems, they go through each day, each trip on the open rails, with no apparent concern. If you want to know the truth, sometimes we brakemen would envy them because they didn't seem to have a care in the world."

"Dad, were you ever afraid of running into these characters while you were working in the yards?" I asked.

"Not really. At least, not the hobos. I was a lot younger then, and as a brakeman, we needed to be pretty fit to do that job. We brakemen were used to taking care of ourselves in the yards or out on the main line.

"Son, just like in all walks of life, there is a 'caste system,' and that's also true in hobo society. Where you fall into this system is based on an individual's personal courage, physical strength, and cleverness.

"The common railroad hobo lives as I just described. He is seldom guilty of any crime or violence. In some cases, the railroads don't even care about the hobos and permit them to ride for free. As you can imagine, these men are, of course, friendly and entertaining. But you can never tell.

"Some hoboes, accustomed to getting used to free transportation, can get ugly and vengeful when they get put off the train.

"Son, communities and the railroads often live in two different worlds. Municipalities can be quite selfish in dealing with hobos and tramps. Many a tramp who has been picked up is re-leased from police custody on the condition that he leave town. And it is no surprising thing for a cop to bring a hobo or tramp down to the freight yard and bribe a trainman to 'carry' the shiftless wayfarer to any point wherever.

"If a train employee puts the fellow off the train in one community, the same thing is likely going to happen again the next day.

"All trainmen understand that we have to be careful about how we handle these men. Unfortunately, society looks upon their local police force differently than they look at railroad employees.

He could tell by the look on my face that I didn't understand.

"Let's say a local cop roughs up a tramp. Nobody cares, for he is one of the 'undesirables', and 'good riddance' to him and his kind. The idea is to take him to the rail yard and be done with him.

"But if they observed a railroad employee doing the same thing to a man who has stolen a free ride on the rails, a jury might overlook that the bum is a railroad trespasser. Worse, they may see this man as an abused victim of an oppressive big railroad corporation and award a healthy settlement to him. So there is often a tension between views of the towns and the railroads. Because of that, the never-ending 'floating population' of Hobos and Tramps continues.

"There is one group that I haven't told you about. These are the yeggmen.

"A yeggman is a much more dangerous character. If you talk to any trainman or railroad detective, they'll tell you that the yeggmen, who also ride the rails, are responsible for much of the crime in this country. These are not merely down-on-their-luck beggars, but clever and experienced burglars and hold-up men as well.

"These yeggmen look down with contempt on the common hobo or tramp, even though they often travel together on the rails. Yeggmen have been around for many years, and they have adapted their tactics a great deal over time.

"Used to be that a 'yegg' carried a set of tools for breaking into safes and vaults; but these days, these guys use high explosives and seldom or never found carrying common burglar tools. They are incredibly bold too! Even though explosions at robberies sites are loud and awaken the neighbors, the yegg burglars tend to remain around the scene until they get what they are after, even though they often risk getting caught in the act.

"Then their truly dangerous side appears. They have no hesitation in opening fire on anyone who disturbs them.

"Because of the way they dress, they look like the common hobo. The difference though is that even though they blend in with the hobo community, they have no regard for human life.

"These dangerous men like to use explosives in their robberies. They break into railroad storehouses to steal the dynamite and nitroglycerine that is commonly used by railroad construction crews. What's worse is the average yeggman would have no problem killing a railroad cop or brakeman. In fact, doing so raises him in the esteem of his criminal associates. Like I said, these are very bad men."

I always knew Dad's job was dangerous, but I had no idea what he had to deal with every day on the job. But my curiosity had no bounds, and I pleaded with Dad to tell me more.

"Besides safe and vault burglary," he continued, "these yeggmen go from city to city, jumping off trains and engaging in house and highway robbery. They're always on the lookout for opportunities, and once a job is completed, they quickly fence their ill-gotten gains before getting out of town on the next train."

By this time, my eyes were as wide as saucers.

"How can you tell if it's a yeggman?" I asked.

"If you hang around a hobo camp, and you better not, you might hear some unfamiliar language in a camp where there are yeggs. Yeggs have their own peculiar slang that helps identify them. They use language that the common hobo does not.

"They refer to a prison as 'dump,' dynamite or nitroglycerine is called 'soup,' 'oil,' or 'grease,' and high explosives operators are called 'boxmen' or 'shotmen.' And, 'Cats' are the local beggars the yegg uses for menial tasks around camp or to fence their stolen goods. Cats are not involved in the actual robberies, but the yegg gives them a cut of the proceeds for fencing the stolen goods to the public. Many of these 'Cats' see themselves as apprentices that hope to become yeggs someday.

"Notorious criminals, yeggs are seldom known by their correct names. They use nicknames given to them by others or ones they adopted themselves. Their 'road name' usually reflects some personal peculiarity or their former place of residence. For example, a red-haired yegg from Denver would be known as 'Colorado Red.' Some of the road names that appear on flyers put up by the Pinkerton Detective Agency include 'Frisco Slim,' 'Michigan Fats,' 'Topeka Banjo,' 'The Frog,' 'Olean Flyer,' 'Chicago Irish' and many others like that."

Dad continued, saying, "These roadmen even have an ingenious system for keeping track of one another's movements and whereabouts."

He pointed to a nearby work shed that had hand-drawn writing on it.

"If you pay close attention to what you see on rail yard water tanks, worksheds, outhouses, switch-shanties, and in even the restrooms of railway stations, these itinerants use a shorthand understood by the professional hobo, tramp, and yegg. That's how these men keep track of who is going where.

Shorthand Used by Hobos and Tramps

"They write or carve a short message that includes what each calls his 'road name' and the date and the direction in which he is going. So 'Pete W, 4-19-49 W' shows that Petersburg Whitey was there on April 19, 1949, and went west, and 'Chi. Frk, 3-20-51 S' tells the story that Chicago Frank was here on March 20, 1951, and went south.

"Generally, when a hobo gets to his next stop, he'll head to the nearest hobo encampment, but not the yeggs. The yeggs who travel from city to city will first head to one of the local 'hang-outs' where they associate with other yeggs and figure out the local 'action'". These hangouts are usually in some low-life saloon or cheap boarding house, run by the proprietor, who may have been a yeggman himself. There is a criminal fraternity among yeggmen and they seem to be very loyal to each other.

"They are 'most wanted' men that have committed murders, burglaries, and other major crimes. Large rewards have been offered for information leading to their capture. That's why they stick together. Honor among thieves, I guess you could say."

"So, they're hard to catch?" I asked.

"Oh yes, they are very hard to catch. Because they know how to hide amidst the hobo community. It's very frustrating to law enforcement when trying to locate and arrest them. They are masters of deception; remember that these are not stupid or illiterate people but clever and cunning career criminals.

"They also often carry falsified identification cards showing them to be members of one of the many labor organizations of today. When they have these fake credentials, they can travel as members of the brotherhoods of trainmen, switchmen, stonecutters, printers, etc. If arrested or questioned by an officer or a trainman, they produce their traveling cards and pretend to be honest workingmen, simply traveling to the next place to find work. This tactic works pretty well and frequently keeps them from being arrested.

"As I mentioned, yeggs are also masters of disguise who blend in with the hobo community. A yeggman may have amassed significant wealth because of their thievery acts, but the average successful yegg will make very few changes in his personal appearance or attire. So, he usually looks like an ordinary out of work laborer, blending in with the masses, and avoiding unwanted attention.

"This is where the yegg differs from the run-of-the-mill burglar. After a successful heist, today's burglars often start living the 'high life,' living conspicuously and often dressed in the height of fashion. Yeggs don't hang around the 'common' local criminal. They consider themselves a special breed who has mastered the art of staying in the shadows."

By this time, it was getting late, and Dad said we needed to head back home. Tomorrow was a school day, after all. On the trip back home, I didn't have a word to say, but now had millions of images running through my mind.

As Dad described these men in great detail, I came to understand his daily routine as a brakeman. He came in contact with these men and knew exactly the right thing to do when coming face to face with one. Up to this point, I had never seen my dad as daring as a high-wire acrobat or a high-stakes negotiator. But in fact, his job was just as dangerous, maybe more.

As I settled into bed and he tucked me in for the night, I pondered the priceless first-hand education that I had received: An education that appears in no textbook. My last thought before dozing off was about all the things I feared; the dark, getting robbed, the death of a parent, and, of course, monsters. I never realized until that very moment that my dad, the brakeman, had to deal with strange things, people in the dark, and true human monsters. If he wasn't paying close attention, many of these things he had shared with me could certainly have resulted in serious injury or death; just as certainly as being cut in half while switching railcars.

A peaceful smile crossed over my face as I faded off into dreamland. My love and appreciation of my dad went through the roof. He had made a life for his family by using a very special set of skills needed to survive in dangerous high-risk situations on the railroad, where one misstep or misjudgment could get a fellow killed.

The End

GLOSSARY

Automatic Air Brake. A railway brake power braking system with compressed air as the operating medium

Atchison Topeka & Santa Fe. Was one of the larger railroads in the United States. The railroad was chartered in February 1859 to serve the cities of Atchison and Topeka, Kansas, and Santa Fe, New Mexico.

Automatic Air Brake. A railway power braking system with compressed air as the operating medium

ATSF. See Atchison Topeka & Santa Fe

B and O. See Baltimore and Ohio Railroad

Baltimore and Ohio Railroad. Was the first common carrier railroad and the oldest railroad in the United States, with its first section opening in 1830.

Baggage Cart. A four wheel wagon that was used to transport luggage from passenger coaches to the station area.

Baldwin Locomotive Works. Was an American manufacturer of railroad locomotives from 1825 to 1951. Originally located in Philadelphia, it moved to nearby Eddystone, Pennsylvania, in the early 20th century.

Ballast. Forms the track bed upon which railroad ties (sleepers) are laid. It is packed between, below, and around the ties. It is used to bear the load from the railroad ties, to facilitate drainage of water, and also to keep down vegetation that might interfere with the track structure

Box Car. A railroad car that is enclosed and generally used to carry freight.

Brakeman. The brakeman was a member of

a railroad train's crew responsible for assisting with braking a train when the conductor wanted the train to slow down or stop. The brakeman was a member of a railroad train's crew responsible for assisting with braking a train when the conductor wanted the train to slow down or stop. A brakeman's duties also included providing flag protection from following trains if the train were to stop, ensuring that the couplings between cars were properly set, lining switches, and signaling to the train operators while performing switching operations. Setting and lining switches, and signaling to the train operators while performing switching operations.

Cab. The crew compartment of a steam or diesel locomotive that houses the train/engine driver, and fireman

Caboose. A car on a freight train for use of the train crew; usually the last car on the train

20th Century Limited. An express passenger train on the New York Central Railroad

(NYC) that ran from 1902 to 1967 between Grand Central Terminal in New York City and LaSalle Street Station in Chicago, Illinois, along the railroad's "Water Level Route".

Canadian Pacific Railway. Was formed to physically unite Canada and Canadians from coast to coast and the building of the railway is considered to be one of Canada's greatest feats of engineering.

Conductor. A train crew member responsible for operational and safety duties that do not involve actual operation of the train/locomotive. The conductor ensures that the train follows applicable safety rules and practices, stays on schedule starting from the stations, sells and checks passenger tickets, ensuring that any cars and cargo are picked up and dropped off properly. The conductor completes in-route paperwork, and directs the train's movement while operating in reverse.

Conrail. Was the primary Class I railroad in

the Northeastern United States between 1976 and 1999.

Continuous Welded Rail. A long, continuous rail formed by welding many short rails.

Coupler. A coupling (or a coupler) is a mechanism typically placed at each end of a railway vehicle that connects them together to form a train.

Cowcatcher. A cowcatcher, also known as a pilot, is the device mounted at the front of a locomotive to deflect obstacles on the track that might otherwise damage or derail it or the train.

Cutting Cars. Taking cars out of a train, or adding cars into a train. Also known as setting out / picking up cars.

Delaware Lackawanna & Western Railroad. Was a U.S. Class 1 railroad that connected Buffalo, New York, and Hoboken, New Jersey, a distance of 395 miles.

Denver and Rio Grande Railway. Was an

American Class I railroad company. The railroad started as a 3 foot narrow-gauge line running south from Denver, Colorado, in 1870.

Derailment. A train coming off the railway tracks.

Draw Hook and Chain. An early method of coupling rail cars. Made obsolete by automatic couplers.

Driving Wheels. The driving wheels of a steam locomotive support the weight of the locomotive and transfer linear force from the pistons into rotational force applied to the rails.

Engineer. The person who operates a railroad locomotive.

Engine Man. A person who operates or helps to operate an engine or locomotive.

Erie Railroad. Was a railroad running between New York City, Buffalo, and Chicago, through the southern counties of New York

State and skirting Lake Erie. It was incorporated in 1832 as the New York and Erie Railroad Company, to build from Piermont, N.Y., on the west bank of the Hudson River, to Dunkirk on Lake Erie. The track was completed in 1851.

Express Car. A railroad car used in passenger-train service for carrying mail, baggage, or express.

Extra Telegraph Operator. An "on call" telegraph operator, brought in as needed for high-traffic situations.

Firemen. A person whose occupation it is to tend the fire for powering a steam engine, which may involve shoveling fuel, typically coal, into the boiler's firebox.

Flag Stop. A stop or station at which the train stops only on request; that is, only if there are passengers or freight to be picked up or dropped off.

Flange Way. The gap in a railroad track that

allows the wheel flange of a railcar or locomotive to pass. See frog or switch.

Freight Cars. A railroad car that is used for carrying goods / material as opposed to people (passenger car).

Frog. The intersection of two rails of a switch.

Grade. The rate of rise or fall of track elevation.

Great Northern Railway. The Great Northern Railway was an American Class I railroad. Running from Saint Paul, Minnesota, to Seattle, Washington, it was the creation of 19th-century railroad entrepreneur James J. Hill and was developed from the Saint Paul & Pacific Railroad.

Guard Rails. Guard rails or check rails are rails used in the construction of the track, placed parallel to regular running rail to keep the wheels of rolling stock in alignment to prevent derailment.

Hamilton Railroad Watch. A compact, clear,

and accurate railroad pocket watch without a cover became essential for safe railroad operation. When up trains and down trains were led onto turnouts and rails were cleared to allow the passage of express trains, train safety depended on punctuality and the exact synchronization of the watches that were carried by the engineers and conductors on the trains and railroad workers in the field.

Heavyweight Pullman Car. A heavyweight car is one that is physically heavier than a lightweight car due to its construction. While early cars used wood construction, Pullman switched to heavyweight riveted steel construction in 1910.

Hobo. A hobo is a migrant worker in the United States.

Hobo Camp. A place where hoboes camp.

Hopper Car. A type of railroad freight car used to transport loose bulk commodities such as coal, ore, grain, and track ballast.

Hostler. A train driver, a type of railroad engineer who moves locomotives in and out of service facilities.

Stalls. A space within a roundhouse structure where a single locomotive can be stored. (see roundhouse)

"Blue Coal" Freight. A special freight train designated to haul Anthracite (Blue Coal) from mines to various destinations.

Jimmy Car. A small hopper car used to transport coal from mines

Lantern. Railroad lanterns served a very important purpose, communicating signals between trains and stations. These lanterns featured a glass globe cemented to the metal armature so that it could not be readily removed from the frame.

Liberty Limited. A named train on the Pennsylvania Railroad that ran from Washington D.C. to Chicago, Illinois, through Baltimore, Harrisburg and Pittsburgh.

Locomotive. A locomotive or engine is a railroad unit that provides the motive power to pull a train.

Mail Bag. A railroad mail pouch made of an extra tough canvas material metal rings on each end so the pouch could attach to the arm of a railway mail bag crane. Designed to be snatched by a passing train's mail hook without having to stop to pick up outbound mail.

Main Line. A track extending through yards and between stations which must not be occupied without authority or protection.

Main Line Right Of Way. A strip of land that is granted, through an easement or other mechanism, for transportation purposes.

Milk Train. A special train (express train) with a delivery schedule avoiding need for additional cooling of milk during transit.

Modest Grade. For freight trains, gradients should be as gentle as possible, preferably below 1.5%.

Morse Code. American Morse Code — also

known as Railroad Morse—is the latter-day name for the original version of the Morse Code developed in the mid-1840s.

Nickel Plate Line. The New York, Chicago & St. Louis Railroad Company, popularly known as the "Nickel Plate Road" (reporting mark NKP), had a storied 83-year existence. Starting as a single road from Chicago to Buffalo to compete with the New York Central's Lake Shore and Michigan Southern line.

Norfolk and Western. The Norfolk and Western Railway, was a US class I railroad, formed by more than 200 railroad mergers between 1838 and 1982, headquartered in Roanoke, Virginia.

Norfolk and Western 611. Norfolk & Western 611 is a 4-8-4 "Class J" steam locomotive and perhaps the most advanced such Northern ever built.

Oregon Railroad and Navigation Company. Was a railroad that operated a rail network of

1,143 miles running east from Portland, Oregon, United States, to northeastern Oregon, northeastern Washington, and northern Idaho. It operated from 1896 as a consolidation of several smaller railroads.

Parlor Car. An extra-fare railroad passenger car for day travel equipped with individual chairs.

Pennsylvania Railroad. Established in 1846, headquartered in Philadelphia. By 1882, the Pennsylvania Railroad had become the largest railroad (by traffic and revenue), the largest transportation enterprise, and the largest corporation in the world. Its budget was second only to the U.S. government.

Pinkerton Detectives. The Pinkerton agency first made its name in the late-1850's for hunting down outlaws and providing private security for railroads.

Platform. An area alongside a railway track providing convenient access to trains.

Priority Track Rights. Permission given by

a dispatcher for one train to have priority access to a section of track over another deemed less important.

Putting Trains Together. See cutting cars.

Rail Cars. A non-self-propelled vehicle designed for and used on railroad tracks.

Rail Terminal. The principal stations or a station along a railroad mainline where the train stops only on a signal.

Rail Yard. A series of tracks in a rail network for storing, sorting, or loading and unloading railcars and locomotives.

Railroad Caller. A person designated to convey important messages to railroad employees.

Railroad Detectives. Persons hired by the railroads (sometimes called "bulls") to keep hoboes off trains, so you couldn't just go to a railroad yard and climb on.

Railroad Station. A building containing accommodations for railroad passengers or freight.

Railroad Store Houses. Where the railroad keeps their supplies and materials for construction, operations and maintenance.

Railroad Telegrapher. An operator who uses a telegraph key to send and receive the Morse code in order to communicate between stations via telegraph wires.

Railroad Ties. A railroad tie, crosstie, railway tie or railway sleeper is a rectangular support for the rails in railroad tracks. Generally laid perpendicular to the rails, ties transfer loads to the track ballast and subgrade, hold the rails upright and keep them spaced to the correct gauge.

Railway Clerk. Company railway clerks relay customer orders to railroads, familiar with routes, timetables and rates.

Refrigerated Railcar. A boxcar that is designed to carry perishable freight at specific temperatures. Reefer railcars are different from insulated boxcars and ventilated boxcars (commonly used for transporting fruit), because neither is fitted with cooling apparatus.

Regulator Clock. A type of clock that was used as the time standard to which all other clocks were set. Regulators were typically installed in places of business, railroad stations, and public buildings and used to schedule work and set other clocks.

Roadbed. The bed on which the ties, rails, and ballast of a railroad rest.

Rolling Stock. Locomotives, cars (passenger, freight, etc.), or other vehicles used on a railroad.

Roundhouse. A circular building for housing and repairing locomotives. Has several "stalls" for storing individual locomotives.

Section Crew. A team that is responsible for repairing and maintaining the track in a particular section (aka Maintenance of Way).

Section Dispatcher. The Railroad is broken into several "Sections" with each section having a Section Dispatcher in charge of it. The Train Dispatcher relays Train Orders, authorities and messages to trains through the Towers in their respective section.

Semaphore Signal. An apparatus for conveying information by means of visual signals.

Short Line. Short lines are smaller railroads that run shorter distances and connect shippers with the larger freight rail network.

Siding. A short railway track beside the main tracks, where engines and carriages are left when they are not being used.

Southern Railway. The Southern Railway was a class 1 railroad based in the Southern United States between 1894 and 1982.

Spike Hammer. A special hammer that enables the operator to drive the spike from over the rail, thus getting both sides without having to cross to the other side.

Spikes. Used to maintain gauge between the

running rails and also they are a means to secure the steel rail to the railroad tie.

Spring Rail Frogs. Used on main lines where the turnout runs are infrequently used. Eliminating the open flangeway in the turnout run reduces impact and where at the point, and provides smoother operation in the mainline.

Station Agent. The man in charge of a railroad station. In smaller towns, this job also included being ticket agent, baggage handler and telegraph operator.

Steam Locomotive. A locomotive that provides the force to move itself and other vehicles by means of the expansion of steam.

Streamlined Locomotive. A style of engine design providing increased efficiency through reduction of wind resistance.

Switchback. A method of climbing steep gradients with minimal need for tunnels and heavy earthworks

Switch Lamps. A type of lantern typically

used on principal tracks in railroad yards or on main routes in the vicinity of junctions or stations.

Switch Points. Are used to divert rolling stock from one track to another.

Switch Shanty. A switchman's shelter and a center of communication in the middle of busy rail yards.

Switches. A railroad switch, (or turnout), is a mechanical installation enabling railway trains to be guided from one track to another, such as at a railway junction or where a spur or siding branches off.

Telegraph Sounder. A device that converts electrical pulses (telegraph signals) into audible sounds and are used to receive Morse code messages.

Tender. A special rail vehicle hauled by a steam locomotive containing the locomotive's fuel (wood, coal, or oil) and water.

Throttle. A handle that starts or moves a locomotive on a train, and serves as a "gas pedal" like with an automobile.

Ticket Auditor. A person that reviews the fiscal affairs of agents and conductors.

Time Table. The authority for the movement of regular trains subject to the rules. It may contain classified schedules and includes special instructions.

Torpedo. An explosive cap fastened to the top of the rail and exploded by the pressure of a rolling wheel to give an audible indication of conditions on the track ahead.

Track Crew. Crew of track laborers assigned to maintenance work at various points on a railroad right-of-way.

Track Derailing Devices. A device used to prevent fouling (blocking or compromising) of a rail track (or collision with anything present on the track, such as a person, or a train) by unauthorized movements of trains or unattended rolling stock. The device works by derailing the equipment as it rolls over or through it.

Track Joint. A connection between two tracks consisting of two points and a short piece of track in between.

Track Work. Construction or maintenance of railroad tracks.

Tractive Effort. The amount of tractive effort that must be produced by the motive power to start moving a train from a dead stop without slipping the wheels.

Trainman. A member of the crew that operates a railroad train.

Trainmaster. Person in charge of the trains operating in a division or subdivision of a railroad.

Train Orders. An order issued by or through a proper railway official to govern the movement of trains.

Train Signals. Used to direct the movement of Trains to avoid collisions and bottlenecks.

Tramp. A migratory non-worker.

Trestle. A braced framework of timbers, piles, or steelwork for carrying a railroad over a depression.

Truss Rods. Rods supporting freight car underframes.

Vestibule. Doorways on either side of passenger cars to allow passenger egress at stations, a door into the body of the car, and, at the end of the car, a doorway to allow access to the next car through a flexible gangway connection.

Watchman's Shanty. A small structure with a window designed to provide the watchman a view of the tracks and crossing.

Water Tank. A water stop or water station on a railroad is a place where steam trains stop to replenish water.

Way Bill. A shipping document listing the goods sent by a common carrier, such as a railroad, and including charges.

Yeggman. A burglar or safe-break.

RESOURCES

A Brief Description of the Canals and Rail Roads of the United States (1834), Henry Schenck Tanner

A Catechism of the Steam Engine in Its Various Application to Mines, Mills, Steam Navigation, Railways, and Agriculture (1869), John Bourne

A Description of the Canals and Rail-roads of the United States Comprehending Notices of All the Works of Internal Improvements (etc.) (1856), H.S. Tanner

A History of the Railway Mail Service (1905), Columbian Correspondence College (Washington, D.C.)

A Manual of the Principles and Practice of Road-Making: Comprising the Location, Construction and Improvement of Roads and Railroads (1872) W. M. Gillespie

A Practical Treatise on Rail-roads and Carriages (1825), Thomas Tredgold

A Practical Treatise on the Construction and Formation of Railways, Second Edition (1861) James Day (Engineer)

A Textbook of Railroad Engineering (1898), International Correspondence Schools

A Textbook on Electric Lighting and Railways (1901)

A Treatise on Machine-Tools, Etc. as Made by Wm. Sellers & Co. -- Manufacturers of Machinists' Founders', Smiths', and Boiler-Makers' Tools, Shafting and Mill Gearing, Railway Turning and Transfer Tables, Pivot Bridges, Etc (1880

A Treatise on the Steam Engine in Its Application to Mines, Mills, Steam Navigation, and Railways (1864, 1875), John Bourne

A Treatise on Wooden Trestle Bridges According to the Present Practice on American Railroads (1892) Wolcott Cronk Foster

Alaska Railroad Record (1919)

American Engineer and Railroad Journal (1897, 1898)

American Inland Waterways, Their Relation to Railway Transportation and to the National Welfare (1910), Herbert Quick

American Railroad Journal (1855, 1854, 1882)

American Railroad Journal and Mechanics' Magazine (1857, 1858)

Anecdotes for the Steamboat and Railroad (1853)

Buildings and Structures of American Railroads (1894) Walter Gilman Berg

Bulletin - American Railway Engineering Association (1903) American Railway Engineering Association

Bulletin of the International Railway Association (1896), International Railway Association

Bulletin of the International Railway Congress Association (1896), International Railway Congress Association

Catalogue of Freight Train Brakes (1888), American Brake Company, St. Louis

Catalogue of the Hopkins Railway Library (1895), Stanford University. Libraries, Frederick John Teggart

Classification of Train-miles, Locomotive Miles and Car-Miles for Steam Roads. (1908) United States. Interstate Commerce Commission

Clegg's Patent Atmospheric Railway (1856)

Confessions of a Book Agent; Or, Twenty

Years by Stage and Rail (1906), James Howard Mortimer

Constitution of the Brotherhood of Railroad Freight Handlers (1911), Brotherhood of Railroad Freight Handlers

Construction of Railroads in Alaska (1913), United States. Congress. Senate. Committee on Territories

Copy of the Acts Incorporating the Sandusky, Toledo & Michigan City Rail Road Company, with the Report of the Survey of the Road by John Hopkins, Esq (1870)

Efficient Railway Operation (1919), Henry Stevens Haines

Engineering News and American Railway Journal (1890, 1891, 1893, 1895, 1896, 1890, 1896)

Engineering Problems in Electric Elevated and Suburban Railroading (1901), Frank Julian Sprague

Erie Railway (1890) New York, Lake Erie & Western Railroad

Explanation of Train Rules, Train Orders, Special Instructions, and Rules Governing the Use of Block Signals and Interlocking Plants (1920), Otho William Brandt

Freight Terminals and Trains (1913) John Albert Droege

General Catalogue of Electric Light, Railway, Telephone and House Supplies (1917), Electric Appliance Company

General Rules and Regulations of the Eastern Railroad and Divisions (1872) Eastern Railroad Company

General Specifications for Iron and Steel Railroad Bridges and Viaducts (1892), Theodore Cooper

General Specifications for Steel Railroad Bridges and Viaducts. New and Rev. Ed. (1906, 1907), Theodore Cooper

Green Bay, Milwaukee and Chicago Rail Road

(1865) Green Bay, Milwaukee and Chicago Rail Road,C. R. Alton

Guide to the National Exposition of Railway Appliances, Chicago. (1886), National exposition of railway appliances

Handbook and Catalogue of the Railway Appliances Manufactured (1922), William Henry Miner

Herapath's Railway Journal (1856)

Historical Sketch of the Illinois Central Railroad (1892), William K. Ackerman

History of a Line (Colorado Midland Railway.) (1891), Horace A. Bird

History of Elmira, Horseheads and the Chemung Valley, with Sketches of the Churches, Schools, Societies, Rail Roads, Manufacturing Companies, Etc., (1876), Galatian, A.B. & Co

History of Express Companies and American Railroads (1859), Alexander Lovett Stimson

History of the Chesapeake and Ohio Railroad (1876), Chesapeake and Ohio Railroad Company

History of the Chicago, Milwaukee & St. Paul Railway Co. and Representative Employees (1901)

History of the Engineering, Construction and Equipment of the Pennsylvania Railroad Company's New York Terminal and Approaches (1913), William Couper

History of the Express Companies: and the origin of American Railroads. ... Second Edition (1858), A. L. Stimson

History of the Illinois Central Railroad Company and Representative Employees (1902), Railroad Historical Company

Illustrated Catalogue of Railway and Machinists' Tools and Supplies (1895), Manning, Maxwell & Moore, Inc

Illustrated Catalogue of Railway, Steamship, Machinist, Factory, Mill and Electric Supplies (1902), Manning, Maxwell & Moore, Inc

Illustrated Catalogue of Railway, Steamship, Machinists' & Contractors' Tools & Supplies (1892), Motley, Thornton N., & Co

Industrial Resources of Western Kansas and Eastern Colorado. Kansas Pacific Railway (1878), Richard Smith Elliott

International Railway Journal (1901)

Manual of the Railroads of the United States (1896), Henry Varnum Poor

Manual Training Magazine (1913), Charles Alpheus Bennett, William Thomas Bawden

Modern Examples of Road and Railway Bridges (1878), William Henry Maw, James Dredge

Moody's Manual of Railroads and Corporation Securities (1917, 1927)

Nine Thousand Miles on a Pullman Train (1900), Milton M. Shaw

Official Proceedings of the New York Railroad Club (1895)

Passenger Terminals and Trains (1917), John Albert Droege

Poor's Manual of Railroads (1895, 1902, 1883)

Principles of Locomotive Operation and Train Control (1916), Arthur Julius Wood

Private Freight Cars and American Railways (1910, Louis Dwight Harvell Weld

Proceedings of a National Convention of Railroad Commissioners (1902), National Convention of Railroad Commissioners

Proceedings of the ... Annual Convention of the American Railway Bridge and Building Association (1915), American Railway Bridge and Building Association. Convention

Proceedings of the ... Meeting of the American Society of Railroad Superintendents (1895), American Society of Railroad Superintendents

Proceedings of the American Railway Engineering Association (1919), American Railway Engineering Association

Proceedings of the Boston & Oswego Railroad Convention (1878), Boston and Oswego railroad convention

Proceedings of the Meeting of the American Society of Railroad Superintendents (1892), American Society of Railroad Superintendents

Railroad Accounts and Statistics (1924), Charles E. Wermuth

Railroad Age Gazette (1909)

Railroad Construction (1922), Walter Loring Webb

Railroad Curves and Earthwork (1894), Calvin Frank Allen

Railroad Gazette (1892, 1900, 1905, 1901, 1906, 1907

sylvania, and Business Directory of the Representative Business Houses (1893), Hanni-
fan, P.J., & Co

Railway Adventures and Anecdotes (1884),
Richard Pike

Railway Age (1911, 1921)

Railway Age Gazette (1915

Railway and Locomotive Engineering (1899,
1896, 1898)

Railway and Marine News (1931, 1914)

Railway Carmen's Journal (1905)

Railway Charges for the Transportation of
Wool, (1896)

Railway Economy (1850), Dionysius Lardner

Railway Engineering and Maintenance (1921)

Railway Journal (1900)

Railway Line Clearances and Car Dimensions
Including Weight Limitations of Railroads in

the United States, Canada, Mexico and Cuba (1915)

Railway Locomotives and Cars (1858, 1908, 1882, 1886, 1895, 1898)

Railway Maintenance Engineering (1915), William Hamilton Sellew

Railway Master Mechanic (1907)

Railway Mechanical Engineer (1920)

Railway Review (1884, 1895, 1931)

Railway Review (1920)

Railway Signal Engineer (1921)

Railway Signaling and Communications (1913, 1919)

Railway Station Service (1911), Benjamin Chapman Burt

Railway Times (1890, 1899)

Railway Track and Structures (1912, 1916)

Railway World (1891)

Ralph, the Train Dispatcher (1912), Allen Chapman

Sam Johnson: the Experience and Observations of a Railroad Telegraph Operator (1882), John Albert Clippinger

Shape Book Containing Profiles, Tables, and Data Appertaining to Shapes, Plates, Bars, Rails, and Track Accessories Manufactured by Carnegie Steel Company, Pittsburg, Pa (1912), Carnegie Steel Company

Shippers' Guide for Fifty Thousand Express Offices and Railway Stations (1892), Adams Express Company

Standard Specification for Steel Railway Bridges (1933), Canadian Standards Association

Standard Tee Rail Construction for Steam Rail Road and Industrial Railway Track and Switch Work (1921), Lorain Steel Company

Standard Turn-outs on American Railroads (1899), Frederick Augustus Smith

Railroad structures (1897), International Correspondence Schools

The Finest Train in the World (1888), Union Pacific Railway Company

The Manual of the Railway Signal Association (1913), Railway Signal Association

The Need of Automatic Train Control (1921), Walter Mason Camp

The Official Guide of the Railways and Steam Navigation Lines of the United States, Porto Rico, Canada, Mexico and Cuba (1900, 1904, 1912, 1908)

The Official Railway Equipment Register (1919)

The Official Railway Guide (1902, 1883, 1889, 1894, 1902

The Organization and History of the Chicago, Milwaukee & St. Paul Railway Company (1894), John W. Cary

The Problem of Motive Power Under the National Administration of Railroads (1918), Alba Boardman Johnson

The Railroad and Engineering Journal (1890)

The Railroad Era (1888), Horatio Allen

The Railroad Signal Dictionary (1908), Railway Signal Association

The Railroad Telegrapher (1902, 1918, 1905, 1909, 1913, 1914)

The Railroad Trainman (1899, 1891, 1899), Daniel L. Cease

The Railway Age (1904, 1910, 1896, 1904, 1905, 1907)

The Railway Age and Northwestern Railroader (1901)

The Railway Agent and Station Agent (1901, 1892)

The Railway and Engineering Review (1902, 1907, 1910), Walter Mason Camp

The Railway Auditor (1902), Herbert Clarkson Whitehead

The Railway Clerk (1905, 1923)

The Railway Conductor (1899, 1892, 1908)

The Railway Engineer (1890, 1901), Lawrence Saunders, S. R. Blundstone

The Railway Library (1912), Slason Thompson

The Railway Magazine, and Annals of Science (1856)

The Railway News (1891, 1880, 1890)

The Railway Review (1921)

The Railway World (1906)

The Standard Code of the American Railway Association (1913), American Railway Association

The Story of the Rome, Watertown and Ogdensburgh Railroad (1922), Edward Hungerford

The Transition Spiral, Earthwork, Railroad Location, Trestles, Trackwork, Railroad Buildings and Miscellaneous Structures, Highways, Pavements, City Surveying, City

Streets, Construction Drawing (1908), International Correspondence Schools

The Why and How of Interurban Railways (1906), Guy Morrison Walker

The World's Rail Way (1896), Joseph Gladding Pangborn

Train Dispatchers Bulletin (1915)

Train Operation by Signal Indication (1921), Henry Muhlenberg Sperry

Triple Articulated Compound Locomotive for the Erie Railroad Company (1915), Baldwin Locomotive Works

Winter Excursion Routes, Pennsylvania Railroad Co. (1902, 1903, 1905)

IMAGE CREDITS

A Second Chance

Riding the Truss Rods

Wikipedia, 1894, [Two hobos riding the rods], Wikipedia, licensed under CC BY-ND 2.0.

A Generous Handout
Johnson - Wanted Dead or Alive

A Terrible Train Robber

Stagecoach Robbery

[Outlaws of the Border: A Complete and Authentic History of the Lives of Frank and Jesse James, the Younger Brothers, and Their Robber Companions..], Jay Donald, Jan 1882 · Coburn & Newman Publishing Company

Train Robbery

Screenshot from ''The Great Train Robbery', Edwin S. Porter, 1903

Miner - wanted poster

[Reward Notice for Bill Miner], Reward notice for the recapture of Bill Miner, sent to police departments, publications and private detective agencies, 1907, Library and Archives Canada

Railroad Semaphore Positions

[Semaphore Signals] 1917, Elements of Railroad Engineering, William G. Raymond , C.E. , LLD.

All Aboard The Milk Train
Telegraph Sounder

Elements Of Telegraph Operating Elementary Telegraphy, Telegraphy, Telegraph Repeaters Power Equipment] 1913, International Textbook Company Scranton , Pa

Cooling Collected Milk

[Member of the Dairymen's Cooperative

Creamery, cooling fresh milk in water trough on his farm.], New York Public Library, 1941, Creative Commons CC0 1.0 Universal Public Domain Dedication ("CCO 1.0 Dedication")

Afternoon Milk Delivery

[How Milk Is Marketed] 1898, By Perry Mason & Company, Boston, Mass

Loading the Days Shipment

[Unloading cans of milk from early morning train. Montrose, Colorado], Lee, Russell, 1903-1986, photographer, Farm Security Administration - Office of War Information Photograph Collection (Library of Congress)

I Want To Meet The Engineer

Parlor Car

[Pere Marquette Railroad parlor car no. 30], between 1900 and 1910, Detroit Publishing Company photograph collection (Library of Congress)

Working on Engine in the Roundhouse

[Servicing an engine at the roundhouse at a Chicago and Northwestern Railroad yard],

1942, Jack Delano (Library of Congress - LC-USW3- 012796-D)

611 Engine Coming Through

Author photo collection

Love On A Train

Fighting the Winter Storm

[Information for Employees and the Public], Pennsylvania Railroad, 1914

Curtis

[Man in suit, outdoors], 1910s, Wallach Division Picture Collection, New York Public Library

Terry the Tramp

Jacksonville Waterfront

Sanborn Maps 1900

The Race for Raton Pass

Raton Pass on the Old Santa Fe Trail

Author image

Raton Pass Switchback

Railroad Gazette, June 1879

Switchback and Tunnel Plan

Railroad Gazette, June 1879

Uncle Dick Locomotive

Baldwin Locomotive Works: Illustrated Catalogue of Locomotives, Baldwin Locomotive Works, 1881

Hand Rock Drill

Blasters ' Handbook, E. I. du Pont de Nemours & Company, 1918

The Trackwalker

Track Torpedoes

The Railways of America: Their Construction, Development, Thomas McIntyre Cooley,1890

Watchman's Shanty

Maintenance of Way Cyclopedia, E. T. Howson, 1921, American Railway Engineering Association

Railroad Switch (Turnout)

[The Problem Of Snow Removal] adapted from 1917, By J. W. Powers, Supervisor , New York Central, Railway Maintenance Engineer

Santa Claus On The Train
Mother and Child

[Migrant Mother], 1936, Dorothea Lange, Wikipedia, licensed under CC BY-ND 2.0.

The Spirits Of Tunnel 19
Location of Tunnel 19

[Cairo Quadrangle West Virginia - Ritchie County 7.5 Minute Series (Topographic)], United States Geological Survey. Title. Map. Edition or Series. Reston, Va: U.S. Department of the Interior, 1964

Cowcatcher on a Locomotive

Illustrated Catalogue Of Locomotive, S. Burnham, Parry, Williams & Co., 1881

The Turkey Run
Boxcars on a Siding

123rf

Proposed 3 Section tray

Author image

Family Watching TV

Family watching television, c. 1958, National

Archives and Records Administration, Evert F. Baumgardner

Can't Be Home For Christmas
Coal Car

The Car Builders Dictionary, 1888

The Yeggmen
Hobo Camp

The World According To Hoboes, 1931

Jeff Elliott, Santa Rosa History
Shorthand Used by Hobos and Tramps

The Curse of Tramp Life, Leon Ray Livingston, A-No. 1,1912

ABOUT THE AUTHOR

For most of the past six decades I've been involved with railroads; watching them, working on them, riding in them.

Author 1982

I grew up in a railroad town that served as many as a hundred and fifteen trains per day and the railroads employed a significant part of the area's working population.

I was blessed by knowing many individuals who exposed me to countless dimensions of railroad life. These individuals allowed me to have a very personal experience of trains and railroad life. Being exposed to these people has inspired my career, where one of my first adult jobs was working in a company that for over 100 years provided much of the signaling and switching equipment used by the U.S. railroad industry. Throughout my career I have had different interactions with railroading including the upgrading of systems and procedures for the Railroad Retirement Board in Chicago.

A few years later, I was engaged in the restoration of vintage locomotives and railcars, which led me to a group seeking to revive a historic railroad that went through the heart of Pennsylvania's famous Oil Creek Valley. My bride and I have been delighted to serve as Conductors on steam excursions across several states riding in vintage railcars being pulled by legacy steam locomotives.

In the more recent past, I was invited to serve on the education committee and be a lecturer for The American Railway Engineering and Maintenance-of-Way Association, the North American railway industry group that creates the best practices for the design, construction and maintenance of railway infrastructure.

Over the past twenty years, I have written and told hundreds of stories about the century I call "Industrial America" era. As a professional storyteller, I have told my stories to dozens of corporate events across the United States and to thousands of people in various groups and organizations here and abroad.

Nancy, my bride of almost four decades, and our beloved cat Lulu continue to be my constant support and inspiration. My life-long journey and love affair with trains which began in upstate New York, through Pennsylvania, D.C., Maryland, and Atlanta, now enables me to enjoy the warm and sunny climate of Tampa, Florida.

In my kitchen, I attempt to recreate the sumptuous and exotic menus of Pullman chefs, but I realize I still am very much a culinary apprentice and my efforts are a work in progress.

Sit back and enjoy my book and come along with me on a journey back to bygone days.

And if you'd like to read or listen to more of my other stories, visit my website at www.Jim-Kissane.com

You can contact me by email at Storyteller@ JimKissane.com